HYPERSANITY
THINKING
BEYOND
THINKING

There are essentially three types of people: those who love life more than they fear it, those who fear life more than they love it, and those who have no clue what I'm talking about.

HYPERSANITY
THINKING BEYOND THINKING

NEEL BURTON

Acheron Press
Flectere si nequeo superos
Acheronta movebo

© Acheron Press 2019

Published by Acheron Press

All rights reserved. No part of this book may be reproduced or transmitted, in any form or by any means, without permission.

A CIP catalogue record for this book is available from the British Library.

ISBN 978-1-913260-00-2

Printed and bound by SRP Limited, Exeter, Devon, UK

Contents

Introduction ix

1.	Arguments	1
2.	Fallacies	7
3.	Questions	13
4.	Answers	25
5.	Enemies	31
6.	Rhetoric	37
7.	Language	49
8.	Languages	59
9.	Reason	67
10.	Intelligence	77
11.	Knowledge	83
12.	Memory	93
13.	Science	105
14.	Truth	115
15.	Intuition	123
16.	Wisdom	131
17.	Inspiration	141
18.	Insight	149
19.	Emotion	153

| 20. | Music | 171 |
| 21. | Imagination | 175 |

Final words	181
Notes	185
Index	199

Introduction

'Hypersanity', or perhaps 'super-sanity', is not a common or accepted term. But neither did I make it up.

I first came across the word while training in psychiatry, in the *Politics of Experience* by RD Laing. In this book, first published in 1967, Laing presented madness as a voyage of discovery that could open out onto a free state of higher consciousness, or hypersanity. For Laing, the descent into madness could lead to a reckoning, to an awakening, to 'breakthrough rather than breakdown'.

A few months later, I read CG Jung's autobiography, *Memories, Dreams, Reflections*, which provided a case in point. In 1913, on the eve of the Great War, Jung broke off his close friendship with Freud, and spent the next few years in a troubled state of mind that led him to a 'confrontation with the unconscious'.

As Europe tore itself apart, Jung gained first-hand experience of psychotic material in which he found 'a matrix of mythopœic imagination which has vanished from our rational age'. Like Gilgamesh, Odysseus, Heracles, Orpheus, and Aeneas before him, he travelled deep down into an abyssal underworld where he conversed with Salome, an attractive young woman, and with Philemon, an old man with a white beard and the wings of a kingfisher. Although Salome and Philemon were products of his unconscious, they had lives of their own and said things that he had not previously thought. In Philemon, Jung had at long last found the father-figure that both Freud and his own father had failed to be. More than that, Philemon was a guru, and prefigured what Jung himself was later to become: the 'wise old man of Zürich'. As the war burnt out, Jung re-emerged into sanity, and considered that he had found in his madness 'the prima materia for a lifetime's work'.

The Laingian concept of hypersanity, though modern, has ancient roots. Once, upon being asked to name the most beautiful of all things, Diogenes the Cynic (d. 323 BC) replied *parrhesia*, which in Ancient Greek means something like 'free speech' or 'full expression'. Diogenes used to stroll around Athens in broad daylight brandishing an ignited lamp. Whenever curious people stopped to ask what he was doing, he would reply, 'I am just looking for a human being'—insinuating that the people of Athens were not living up to, or even aware of, their full human potential.

After being exiled from his native Sinope for having defaced its coinage, Diogenes immigrated to Athens, took up the life of a beggar, and made it his mission to metaphorically deface the coinage of custom and convention, which, he maintained, was the false currency of morality. He disdained the need for conventional shelter or any other such 'dainties' and elected to live in a tub and survive on a diet of onions. Diogenes proved to the later satisfaction of the Stoics that happiness has nothing

Introduction

Figure 1: Diogenes looking for a human being.

whatever to do with a person's material circumstances, and held that human beings had much to learn from studying the simplicity and artlessness of dogs, which, unlike human beings, had not 'complicated every simple gift of the gods'. The term 'cynic' derives from the Greek *kynikos*, which is the adjective of *kyon* or 'dog'. Once, upon being challenged for masturbating in the marketplace, Diogenes replied, 'If only it were so easy to soothe hunger by rubbing an empty belly.' When asked, on another occasion, where he came from, he replied, 'I am a citizen of the world' (*cosmopolites*), a radical claim at the time and the first recorded use of the term 'cosmopolitan'. As he approached death, he asked for his mortal remains to be thrown outside the city walls for wild animals to feast upon. After his death in the city of Corinth, the Corinthians erected to his glory a pillar surmounted by a dog of Parian marble.

Both psychosis and hypersanity place us outside society, making us seem 'mad' to the mainstream. Both states attract a heady mixture of fear and fascination. But whereas mental disorder is distressing and disabling, hypersanity is liberating and empowering.

After reading the *Politics of Experience*, the concept of hypersanity stuck in my mind, not least as something that I might aspire to for myself. But if there is such a thing as hypersanity, the implication is that mere sanity is not all it's cracked up to be, a state of dormancy and dullness with less vital potential even than madness. This I think is most apparent in people's frequently suboptimal—if not frankly inappropriate—responses, both verbal and behavioural, to the world around them.

For Laing,

> The condition of alienation, of being asleep, of being unconscious, of being out of one's mind, is the condition of the normal man. Society highly values its normal man. It educates children to lose themselves and to become absurd, and thus to be normal. Normal men have killed perhaps 100,000,000 of their fellow normal men in the last fifty years.

It is certainly true that most 'normal' people, myself included, make very limited and uncomfortable and sometimes dangerous use of their intellectual and human potential. It is not just that we are irrational but that we lack scope and range, as though we had grown into the prisoners of our arbitrary

Introduction

lives, locked up in our own dark and narrow subjectivity. Unable to take leave of our selves, we hardly look around us, barely see beauty and possibility, rarely contemplate the bigger picture—and all, ultimately, for fear of losing our selves, of breaking down, of going mad, using one form of extreme subjectivity to defend against another, as life, mysterious, magical life, passes us by.

We could all go mad, in a way we already are, minus the promise. But what if there was another route to hypersanity, one which, compared to madness, was less fearsome, less dangerous, and less damaging? What if, as well as a backdoor way, there was also a royal road strewn with petals and sprayed with perfume?

This is a book about thinking, which, astonishingly, is barely taught in formal education. Our culture mostly equates thinking with logical reasoning, and the first few chapters examine logic, reason, their forms, and their flaws, starting with the basics of argumentation. You can even put yourself to the test in Chapters 3 and 4.

But, as I have intimated, thinking is also about much more than logical reasoning, and so the book broadens out to examine concepts such as intelligence, knowledge, and truth, and alternative forms of cognition that our culture tends to overlook and underplay, including intuition, emotion, and imagination.

Hypersanity was never going to be an easy romp, but I have tried to be as clear and concise and relevant as possible in an effort to keep the book open to the broadest readership. The chapters are ordered in a loose progression, building up to a radical conclusion (please don't peek), but can, if you prefer, also stand by themselves. If the book fails to live up to its tall promise, it should at least make you into a better thinker—as writing it did me.

And so you can approach *Hypersanity* as an opportunity to hone your thinking skills, which, in the end, are going to be far more important to your impact and wellbeing than any facts that you could ever learn. As BF Skinner once put it, 'Education is what survives when what has been learnt has been forgotten.'

1
Arguments

Arguments are attempts to persuade by providing reasons (or premises) in support of a particular claim (or conclusion).

Arguments are either deductive or inductive. In a deductive argument, the conclusion follows from the premises as their logical consequence.

> *All dogs are mammals. (Premise 1)*
> *Fluffy is a dog. (Premise 2)*
> *Therefore, Fluffy is a mammal. (Conclusion)*

In an inductive argument, the conclusion is merely supported or suggested by the premises.

> *Whenever I eat hazelnuts, my mouth tingles.*
> *Whenever I eat walnuts, my mouth tingles.*
> *I am allergic to nuts.*

Even when sincere, arguments are often messily made, with premises and conclusions embedded in extraneous material, and presented in any order or none at all. In many cases, a premise or conclusion may be implicit, that is, taken for granted and omitted from the argument.

> *Wuthering Heights is the best book ever written in the English language. Each year for the past ten years, it has received more votes than any other book in our survey of British readers.*

If we were to reconstruct this (flawed) argument, it might run something like this:

> *British public opinion accurately reflects literary merit in the English language. (P1, an implicit, and flawed, premise)*
> *Our survey accurately reflects British public opinion. (P2, another implicit premise)*
> *For the past ten years, Wuthering Heights has topped our survey. (P3)*
> *Therefore, Wuthering Heights is the best book ever written in the English language. (C)*

Parts of arguments are either true or false—unless they are vague or ambiguous, in which case they are indeterminate. But arguments themselves, taken as a whole, are either valid or invalid. An argument is valid if its conclusion is a logical consequence of its premises, regardless of the truth or falsity of the premises, or indeed of the conclusion.

> *All organisms with wings can fly. (P1, False)*
> *Penguins have wings. (P2, True)*
> *Therefore, penguins can fly. (C, False)*

Although the above argument is valid (it 'works'), it is unsound. For an argument to be both valid and sound, all its premises have to be true—and, of course, the conclusion has to follow logically from the premises. In such cases, the conclusion is bound to be true.

> *All mammals are warm-blooded. (P1, True)*
> *Bats are mammals. (P2, True)*
> *Therefore, bats are warm-blooded. (C, True)*

For an inductive argument, the equivalent of soundness is cogency. An inductive argument is cogent if its premises are true and render the truth of the conclusion more or less probable.

If you're having trouble deciding whether the form of a deductive argument is valid or invalid, it can be useful to formulate a parallel argument with exactly the same form, true premises, and an obviously false conclusion.

Argument:

> *Some farmers are landowners.*
> *Some landowners are aristocrats.*
> *Therefore, some farmers are aristocrats.*

Argument in symbol or general form:

> *Some A are B.*
> *Some B are C.*
> *Therefore, some A are C.*

Parallel argument:

> Some insects are herbivores.
> Some herbivores are mammals.
> Therefore, some insects are mammals.

A fallacy is some kind of defect in an argument, whether unintended or intended (with the aim to deceive). A formal fallacy is a deductive argument with an invalid form, such as the one above: the argument is invalid regardless of the truth of its premises. In contrast, an informal fallacy is a defect that can only be identified by an analysis of the content of the argument. One way to think about it, as far as deductive arguments are concerned, is that, whereas formal fallacies are invalid, informal fallacies are unsound.

Common formal fallacies include 'affirming the consequent' and 'denying the antecedent'.

Affirming the consequent (also called converse error) is to infer the converse from the first premise.

> If A, then B.
> B.
> Therefore, A.

> If I have the flu, then I have a fever.
> I have a fever.
> Therefore, I have the flu.

Denying the antecedent (also called inverse error) is to infer the inverse from the original statement.

> *If A, then B.*
> *Not A.*
> *Therefore, not B.*

> *If it snows, Jill works from home.*
> *It's not snowing.*
> *Therefore, Jill is not working from home.*

You get the idea, and the idea is all you need, so let's move on to something a little more entertaining...

2
Fallacies

Informal fallacies, popular with politicians and conmen of all stripes, are frequently found in inductive arguments, and can be very hard to uncover. What follows is a selection of some of the more common or important informal fallacies, with, for each fallacy, a short definition and live example (verbatim examples are referenced in the Notes section at the back of the book).

Red herring is a deliberate attempt to weaken or gloss over an argument by diverting attention away from it or its central tenets.

> — *Critical appraisal of the new Bordeaux vintage would be more objective and meaningful if the wines could be tasted blind.*
> —*Just Bordeaux?*

Straw man is to misrepresent an argument, and then knock it down to score an easy win.

> *He believes we can treat the U.S. economy like one of his casinos and default on our debts to the rest of the world, which would cause an economic catastrophe far worse than anything we experienced in 2008.*

> *If you go with what Hillary is saying, in the ninth month, you can take the baby and rip the baby out of the womb of the mother just prior to the birth of the baby. Now, you can say that that's OK. But it's not OK with me, because based on what she's saying, and based on where she's going, and where she's been, you can take the baby and rip the baby out of the womb in the ninth month on the final day. And that's not acceptable.*

Ad hominem ('to the man') is to attack, not the argument itself, but the person making it.

> *Crooked Hillary Clinton is the worst (and biggest) loser of all time. She just can't stop, which is so good for the Republican Party. Hillary, get on with your life and give it another try in three years!*

Genetic fallacy is to accept or reject an argument on the basis of its proponents or origins.

> *I think the people in this country have had enough of experts, people from organizations with acronyms saying that they know what is best and getting it consistently wrong.*

Appeal to hypocrisy (*tu quoque*, 'you too') is to dismiss an argument on the grounds that its proponent's behaviour is inconsistent with it.

> *I don't buy into your arguments for higher taxation. You yourself have used every trick in the book to minimize your effective tax rate—indeed, the very tricks that you propose to ban.*

Note that *ad hominem*, genetic fallacy, and appeal to hypocrisy are all three closely related.

Appeal to popularity, also called appeal to democracy or consensus fallacy, is to conclude the truth of a proposition on the basis that most or many people believe it to be true.

> *Of course he's guilty: even his own mother has turned her back on him.*

Argument to moderation, also called the Englishman's fallacy, is to argue that the moderate view or middle position must be the right or best one.

> *Half the country favours leaving the European Union, the other half favours remaining. Let's compromise by leaving the European Union but remaining in the Customs Union.*

Bifurcation (false dilemma, false trilemma, etc.) is the presentation of limited alternatives when there are in fact more, creating the false impression that the alternatives presented are either mutually exclusive or collectively exhaustive. Bifurcation is often an attempt to force a Hobson's choice of 'take it or leave it'.

> It's my deal or no deal.
> It's my deal, no deal, or no Brexit at all.

Analogical fallacy is to assume that things that are similar in one or more respects must be similar in all respects.

> Like prisons, mental hospitals feature security officers, high walls and fences, and locked or barred windows. And like prisons, mental hospitals are a form of punishment for deviant behaviour.

Cum hoc ergo propter hoc ('with this, therefore because of this') is to assume that correlation necessarily implies causation.

> Studies have found that people who drink red wine with their meals are, on average, less likely to suffer from heart disease. Therefore, drinking red wine with meals protects against heart disease.

There could in this case be a third factor involved, for example, people who drink red wine with their meals may tend to eat more healthily, or to be less stressed.

Gambler's fallacy is the assumption that the outcome of one or more independent events can influence the outcome of a subsequent independent event.

> June is pregnant with her fourth child. Her first three children are all boys, so this time it's bound to be a girl.

Runaway train is an argument that is used to justify a particular course of action, but which, on its own, would also justify much more drastic action in the same direction.

> *Speed kills. Reducing the speed limit from 30 to 20 mph will reduce the number of fatal road traffic accidents.*

In which case, why not reduce the speed limit to 0 mph?

Argument from ignorance, also called the negative proof fallacy, upholds the truth of a proposition based on a lack of evidence against it, or the falsity of a proposition based on a lack of evidence for it.

> *Of course God exists. How else do you explain life on Earth?*

Argument from ignorance is often used to shift the burden of proving or disproving something onto the other side, when normally this burden rests with the party staking the claim.

Begging the question is to argue in circles, supporting the conclusion by means of itself.

> *I oppose same-sex marriage. Marriage is the union between a man and a woman. Same-sex marriage is not marriage.*

This is more or less equivalent to 'I'm right because I say so'.

3

Questions

In this chapter and the next, you can put your critical thinking skills to the test (or skip to Chapter 5 if disinclined).

The ten questions that follow are in the style of the Thinking Skills Assessment (TSA), an admissions test for a number of university courses, most notably Philosophy, Politics, and Economics (PPE) at Oxford. This single course has produced countless senior politicians including over a dozen British and non-British prime ministers.

In the TSA, you'd be expected to answer each question in an average of just under two minutes.

The answers and their explanations are in the next chapter, so that you can't accidentally peek.

1. We [in the UK] are investing more money than ever before in our healthcare system, both in absolute terms and as a proportion of our national wealth. That is why life expectancy continues to rise. Today, women are living to an average age of 82.8 years, and men 78.8 years.

Which of the following states the flaw in the above argument?

A. Health outcomes in the UK are still poorer than in some other European countries.
B. Life expectancy could have risen even if there had been no increase in health spending.
C. Healthier people can expect to live longer.
D. Life expectancy at birth is also rising.
E. Despite the increased funding, the healthcare system is often criticized for delivering poor patient care.

2. As it is, most academics are involved both in research and in teaching. It would be a good idea to separate these functions, with some academics dedicated solely to research and some solely to teaching. Research academics would then be free to focus on research, and teaching academics on teaching, leading to better research and better teaching.

Which of the following best describes the flaw in the above argument?

    A. It considers that research is more important than teaching.
    B. It ignores the possibility that research and teaching are mutually reinforcing activities.
    C. It assumes that specialization leads to increased productivity.
    D. It fails to recognize that most academics have little interest in teaching.
    E. It neglects that, in future, most teaching will take place online.

3. We should reject the idea that it is just to repay what is owed. Suppose a person lends you a weapon, and, when you prepare to return it, you discover that this person has lost their mind. Surely, in such circumstances, it cannot be right to return the weapon to its owner.

Which of the following states the flaw in the above argument?

- A. It employs an exceptional case to reject a general rule.
- B. It introduces irrelevant material to divert attention from the point being made.
- C. It is supported by its own conclusion.
- D. You could return the weapon at a later time.
- E. You could remove the ammunition before returning the weapon.

4. Every year, violent schizophrenics kill a number of people. The papers are full of such horrific cases. Schizophrenics should not be cared for in the community but detained in perpetuity in secure units. This may deprive them of liberty, but what is liberty compared to life?

Which of the following is the best statement of the flaw in the above argument?

A. The papers over-report killings by schizophrenia sufferers.
B. Not all schizophrenia sufferers are violent or pose a risk to others.
C. Schizophrenia cannot be successfully treated.
D. The liberty of the many can trump the life of a few.
E. People should be presumed innocent until proven guilty.

5. Law school is expensive, time-consuming, and demanding. Instead of going to law school, you should start your own business. By starting your own business, you will get a much better financial return on your money, time, and energy. After three years of building your own business, you will have picked up an invaluable education in how to make money. And if you're successful, you will never have to ask someone for a job again.

Which of the following, if true, would most weaken the above argument?

- A. Most people believe that it is easier to suffer silently than to think creatively.
- B. Most people are frightened of failure.
- C. Many new businesses fail.
- D. Most people who go to law school do so because they are genuinely interested in the law.
- E. A large number of people who go to law school end up starting their own business.

6. A study of 15 overweight women found that each woman experienced significant weight loss after replacing her normal evening meal with a fruit course. For two weeks, each woman kept to her normal diet other than replacing her evening meal with a fruit course. After taking 20 minutes exercise, each woman was entitled to eat as many fruits as desired, of whatever type. After just two weeks, every woman had lost at least four pounds and, in one case, up to 11 pounds. Interestingly, those who ate more than five pieces of fruit appeared to lose more weight than those who ate five or fewer. Despite its small size, this study suggests that replacing the evening meal with a fruit course is a simple and effective way of losing weight.

Which of the following, if true, would most strengthen the above argument?

A. The women adhered strictly to the rules of the study.
B. The women were highly motivated to lose weight.
C. The women hardly ate any fruits before they entered the study.
D. The women exercised regularly before they entered the study.
E. The women were only slightly overweight before they entered the study.

7. The increase in illegal human trafficking is one of the darker sides of globalization. Legalizing prostitution reduces illegal human trafficking. Despite raising overall demand for prostitution, customers will favour legal over trafficked prostitutes, thus reducing the demand for the latter. This is one example of how domestic policies crafted at the country level can still exert an impact on aspects of globalization.

Which of the following is an underlying assumption of the above argument?

A. Legalizing prostitution reduces illegal human trafficking.
B. An increase in overall demand for prostitution will not lead to an overall increase in human trafficking.
C. Globalization has led to an increase in illegal human trafficking.
D. Legalizing prostitution will lead customers to favour legal over trafficked prostitutes.
E. Globalization can be shaped and controlled at the country level.

8. Even if God exists, and even if He had an intelligent purpose in creating humankind, we do not know what this predetermined purpose might be and, whatever it might be, we would rather be able to do without it. Unless we can be free to become the authors of our own purpose or purposes, our lives may have, at worst, no purpose at all, and, at best, only some unfathomable and potentially trivial purpose that is not of our choosing.

Which of the following is an underlying assumption of the above argument?

- A. Having the freedom to choose our own purpose is necessarily better than having a predetermined purpose, whatever it might be.
- B. God does not exist.
- C. For something to have a purpose, it must necessarily have been created with that purpose in mind.
- D. Something that was created with a purpose in mind must necessarily have the same purpose for which it was created.
- E. We should strive to create our own purpose or purposes.

9. Don't be envious. Whenever you come across someone who is better or more successful than you are, you can react with either envy or emulation. Envy is the pain that you feel because others have good things; emulation is the pain that you feel because you yourself do not have them. This is a subtle but critical difference. Unlike envy, which is useless at best and self-defeating at worst, emulation is a good thing because it makes us take steps towards securing good things.

Which of the following best expresses the main conclusion of the above argument?

- A. Emulation is a good thing.
- B. Emulation is better than envy.
- C. Don't be envious.
- D. Whenever you come across someone who is better or more successful than you are, you can react with either envy or emulation.
- E. Both envy and emulation involve pain.

10. Our intellect is like a sighted but lame man riding on the shoulders of a blind giant. Schopenhauer anticipates Freud by effectively equating the blind giant of will to our unconscious drives and fears, of which our conscious intellect may not be entirely or even mostly cognizant. For instance, the most powerful manifestation of will is the impulse for sex. Schopenhauer says that it is the will-to-life of the yet unconceived offspring that draws man and woman together in a delusion of lust and love. But with the task accomplished, their shared delusion fades away and they return to their 'original narrowness and neediness'.

Which of the following is a conclusion that can be drawn from the above argument?

A. The lame man represents our unconscious drives and fears.
B. The blind giant of will is mostly powerless.
C. Schopenhauer inspired the work of Freud.
D. We are mostly driven by our intellect.
E. We are mostly driven by unconscious forces.

4
Answers

1. B

To summarize the argument—always a helpful strategy—life expectancy is rising because more money is being ploughed into healthcare. But it could be that life expectancy would have risen even if there had been no increase in health spending (B) owing to better nutrition, technological developments, and so on. The argument assumes that increased spending on healthcare is improving health outcomes, and that this in turn is increasing life expectancy. Instead, it could be that, despite increased spending, the healthcare system is not in fact delivering better health outcomes, or that better health outcomes are only one of several factors behind the increase in life expectancy. A, D, and E do not really touch upon the argument. For example, the fact that the healthcare system is often criticized for delivering poor patient care (E) need not mean that increased spending on healthcare is not improving overall health outcomes. Finally, that healthier people can expect to live longer (C) serves, if anything, to strengthen the argument, which assumes this to be the case.

2. B

The argument effectively assumes that specialization improves quality (rather than productivity, C). However, in the case of research and teaching, this is not necessarily the case, with many academics gaining a teaching edge from their research and a research edge from their teaching (B). The passage is silent on which of research or teaching it considers more important (A). Finally, while D and E may complicate the separation of functions that is being advocated, they do not touch upon the argument's fundamental flaw.

3. A

The best statement of the flaw in the argument is that it employs an exceptional case to reject a general rule. True, there may be some rare circumstances in which it is best not to (immediately) repay a debt, but this does not mean that repaying a debt is wrong in general or in principle. While the material introduced is highly contrived, it is not, strictly speaking, irrelevant (B). Neither is the argument circular (supported by its own conclusion, C) as in, 'we should reject the idea that it is just to repay what is owed because to repay what is owed is wrong in principle.' D and E merely mitigate the exceptional case, without however pointing to the fundamental flaw in the argument.

Answers

4. B

The most egregious flaw in the argument is that it assumes that schizophrenia-sufferers invariably or generally present a high risk to others. In reality, the vast majority of schizophrenia-sufferers are no more likely to be violent than the rest of the population.

5. D

The argument in a nutshell is that, rather than spending one's resources on attending law school, one should spend them on starting a business, because the returns are better. The argument assumes that people who go to law school are principally motivated by financial gain. But if most people who go to law school do so because they are genuinely interested in the law (D), then that assumption is false. A and B, even if true, would not undermine the argument. In particular, what one can do (or is prepared to do) and what one should do are not necessarily the same. The argument already takes into consideration that many new businesses fail (C). Finally, E, that a large number of law graduates end up starting a business, possibly strengthens the argument.

6. D

The principal problem with the study is that the weight loss could also be explained by the daily exercise. But if the women in the study were already exercising before they entered the study, then it becomes much more likely that it was indeed the dietary change (rather than the exercise) that accounted for the weight loss.

7. B

The argument is as follows. The legalization of prostitution will lead to an overall increase in the demand for prostitution; but, because customers favour legal over trafficked prostitutes, the net effect will be to reduce human trafficking. The assumption here is that, in terms of human trafficking, the increase in demand for prostitution will not outweigh the preference of customers for legal over trafficked prostitutes. A is merely a restatement of the conclusion of the argument. C, D, and E, whether they be facts or assumptions, overlie rather than *underlie* the argument.

8. A

The essence of the argument is that whatever God's predetermined purpose for us might be, we would rather be free to choose our own purpose or purposes. This rests on the assumption that being free to choose our own purpose is necessarily better than having a predetermined purpose, whatever that might be (A). Note, it also rests on the assumption that having a predetermined purpose is incompatible with having the freedom to choose our own purpose—although that is not one of the answer options. B is an explicit hypothesis or concession, not an underlying assumption. C and D are assumptions of the counterargument that not to have a pre-determined purpose is, really, not to have any purpose at all. E is more of an implicit conclusion than an underlying assumption.

9. C

The passage kicks off with an imperative, 'Don't be envious'. The rest of the passage is provided in support of why one should not be envious. Therefore, 'Don't be envious' is the main conclusion of the passage—even if it comes first rather than last.

10. E

The passage contains two propositions, which must be read together to be fully understood. The first proposition, contained in the first sentence, is that we are carried around by our unconscious will (the blind giant)—and so 'mostly driven by unconscious forces' (E). The second proposition, contained in the second sentence, is that our conscious intellect may not be entirely or even mostly cognizant of our unconscious will. We may think that our intellect is in charge, but this is merely a 'delusion' (making D false). The rest of the passage serves merely to illustrate these two propositions. The blind giant of will is anything but powerless (making B false), while, of course, the lame man represents our conscious intellect (making A false). Finally, while the passage does state that Schopenhauer anticipates Freud, one is not entitled to conclude that he actually inspired the work of Freud (C). For example, Freud might never have read, or even heard about, Schopenhauer.

5
Enemies

Formal and informal fallacy are but two of what I call 'the five enemies of rational thought'. The other three enemies, stationed in the rearguard, are self-deception, cognitive bias, and cognitive distortion. These concepts overlap somewhat, so don't strain too hard at their edges.

Self-deception

Whereas formal and informal fallacy are about faulty arguments, self-deception is fundamentally about protecting oneself. As I argued in a book called *Hide and Seek: The Psychology of Self-Deception*, all self-deception can be understood in terms of ego defence. In psychoanalytic theory, an ego defence is one of several unconscious processes that we deploy to diffuse the fear and anxiety that arise when who or what we truly are (our unconscious 'id') comes into conflict with who we think we are or who we think we should be (our conscious 'superego').

To put some flesh onto this, let's take a look at three important ego defences: projection, idealization, and intellectualization. Projection is the attribution of one's unacceptable thoughts and feelings to other people. This necessarily involves repression (another ego defence) as a first step, since unacceptable thoughts and feelings need to be repudiated before they can be detached. Classic examples of projection include the envious person who believes that everyone envies her, the covetous person who lives in constant fear of being dispossessed, and the person with fantasies of infidelity who suspects that her partner is cheating on her.

Idealization involves overestimating the positive attributes of a person, object, or idea while underestimating its negative attributes. More fundamentally, it involves the projection of our needs and desires onto that person, object, or idea. A paradigm of idealization is infatuation, or romantic love, when love is confused with the need to love, and the idealized person's negative attributes are glossed over or even construed as positive. Although this can make for a rude awakening, there are few better ways of relieving our existential anxiety than by manufacturing something that is 'perfect' for us, be it a piece of equipment, a place, country, person, or god.

In intellectualization, uncomfortable feelings associated with a problem are kept out of consciousness by thinking about the problem in cold, abstract, or esoteric terms. I once received a phone call from a junior doctor in psychiatry in which he described a recent in-patient admission as 'a 47-year-old mother of two who attempted to cessate her life as a result of being diagnosed with a metastatic mitotic lesion'. A formulation such as 'who tried to kill herself after being told she is dying of cancer' would have been better English, but all too effective at evoking the full horror of this poor lady's predicament.

Here's another example of intellectualization. An ambitious medical student once asked me whether she ought to take up a career in academic medicine, despite (or so it seemed) having already made up her mind on the matter. After raising some arguments in favour, I raised some arguments against, including that the vast majority of people engaged in medical research never make a significant breakthrough. As she did not seem to be taking this argument on board, I asked her to name just one major breakthrough in psychiatric research in the past fifty years. Instead of naming one, or accepting that there had not been any, she resorted to questioning the definition of a breakthrough and even the value of making one—which may have been legitimate things to do, had she first accepted that there had not been any.

This focus on theoretical notions often belies a sort of 'flight into reason': a harsh reality is thought of in terms of an interesting problem or puzzle, without any appreciation for its emotional content or personal implications. Instead of taking it on board, the person may split hairs over definitions, undermine reasonable assumptions, raise trivial objections, and cloud her mind with nebulous arguments and abstruse minutiae. But by failing to see the bigger picture, she also fails to reach the appropriate conclusion or conclusions—which may hit her very hard in five, ten, or fifty years' time. This, of course, is not good reasoning, but it is a good example of how ego defences, of how fear and insecurity, can cloud our ability to reason, not only altering arguments but even shifting the entire frame of the debate.

One ego defence that has come to infect and paralyse much of contemporary political discourse is displacement. Displacement plays an important role in scapegoating, in which uncomfortable feelings such as anger, frustration, envy, guilt, shame, and insecurity are displaced or redirected onto another, often more vulnerable, person or group. The scapegoats—outsiders, immigrants, minorities, 'deviants'—are then persecuted, enabling the scapegoaters to discharge and distract from their negative feelings, which are replaced or overtaken by a crude but consoling sense of affirmation and self-righteous indignation.

Cognitive bias

A cognitive bias is a mental shortcut or heuristic intended to spare us time, effort, or discomfort—often while reinforcing our self-image or worldview—but at a cost of accuracy or reliability.

For example, in explaining the behaviour of others, our tendency is to overestimate the role of character traits over situational factors—a bias, called correspondence bias, which goes into reverse when it comes to explaining our own behaviour. Thus, if Lena fails to mow the lawn, I indict her with forgetfulness, laziness, or spite; but if I fail to mow the lawn, I absolve myself on the grounds of busyness, tiredness, or inclement weather.

Another important cognitive bias is confirmation bias (also called my-side bias), which is the propensity to search for, notice, and recall only those facts and arguments that are in keeping with our existing beliefs while filtering out those that conflict with them—which, especially on social media, can lead us to inhabit a so-called echo chamber.

Well over a hundred cognitive biases have been recognized, and one could write a whole book about them (Please do, I'd read it).

Cognitive distortion

Cognitive distortion is a concept from cognitive-behavioural therapy, developed by psychiatrist Aaron Beck in the 1960s and used in the treatment of depression and other mental disorders. Cognitive distortion involves interpreting events and situations so that they conform to and reinforce our outlook or frame of mind, typically on the basis of very scant or partial evidence, or even no evidence at all.

Common cognitive distortions in depression include selective abstraction and catastrophic thinking. Selective abstraction is to focus on a single negative event or condition to the exclusion of other, more positive ones, for example: 'My partner hates me. He gave me an annoyed look three days ago.' This is similar to confirmation bias, but much more pronounced and pathological.

Catastrophic thinking is to exaggerate the negative consequences of an event or situation, for example: 'The pain in my knee is only going to get worse. When I'm reduced to a wheelchair, I won't be able to go to work and pay the mortgage. So I'll end up losing my house and dying in the street.'

A cognitive distortion can open up a vicious circle: the cognitive distortion aliments the depression, which in turn aliments the cognitive distortion.

Cognitive distortion as broadly understood is not limited to depression and other mental disorders, but is also a feature of, among others, poor self-esteem, jealousy, and marital or relationship conflict.

We'll return to reasoning in Chapter 9, after three chapters on language. Language may not be the same as thought, but it is, at the very least, the general means by which thought is expressed and conveyed.

6
Rhetoric

Attempts to persuade may be argumentative or non-argumentative. Non-argumentative means of persuasion include making eyes, brushing hands, and putting a good meal onto the table. But much more common, especially in the public sphere, is the use of rhetoric, which is the art of persuasive speaking or writing. Barack Obama got himself elected and re-elected to the White House less by the force of his arguments than by his formidable rhetorical skills. The basis of his famous 'Yes we can' shtick, for example, is the rhetorical device of epistrophe (see later).

Rhetorical devices are also poetic devices that can be used to beautify as well as to persuade. Politics aside, rhetorical devices underlie all our favourite poems and songs and expressions.

A few years ago, I wrote a compendium of the most important or effective rhetorical devices and managed to classify them into just eight groups: sound repetition, word repetition, idea or structure repetition, unusual structure, language games, opposition and contradiction, circumlocution, and imagery. I'll take you through those eight groups and try to explain the psychology of each one. Examples used are referenced at the back of the book.

Figure 2: Winston Churchill makes his VE Day broadcast from the Cabinet office in Whitehall, 8 May 1945.

1. Sound repetition

The repetition of a sound or sounds can produce a pleasing sense of harmony. It can also subtly link or emphasize important words or ideas. There are two major forms of sound repetition: consonance and alliteration.

Consonance is the repetition of the same consonant sound, as in, for example,

> *Rap rejects my tape deck, ejects projectile/*
> *Whether Jew or gentile I rank top percentile*

Alliteration is a form of consonance involving the same consonant sound at the beginning of each word or stressed syllable.

> *Curiosity killed the cat*

Sibilance is a form of consonance involving the repetition of sibilant sounds such as /s/ and /sh/. Sibilance is calming and sensual, whereas alliteration on a hard sound produces an entirely different effect.

> *And the silken sad uncertain rustling of each purple curtain...*

Resonance in contrast refers to richness or variety of sounds in a line or passage.

> *Created half to rise, and half to fall*
> *Great lord of all things, yet a prey to all;*
> *Sole judge of truth, in endless error hurl'd:*
> *The glory, jest, and riddle of the world!*

2. Word repetition

Word repetition can create alliteration, rhythm or continuity, emphasis, connection, and progression.

Words can be repeated in several ways.

Most obviously, a word can be repeated in immediate succession (epizeuxis), as in, for example:

> *O dark, dark, dark, amid the blaze of noon*

Or it can be repeated after one or two intervening words (diacope) or at the beginning and end of a clause or line (epanalepsis).

> *Bond, James Bond*
>
> *The king is dead, long live the king!*
>
> *Romeo, Romeo, wherefore art thou my Romeo?*

Or it can be carried across from one clause or line to the next, with the word that ends one clause or line beginning the next (anadiplosis). This brings out key ideas and their connection, imbuing the proposition with something like the strength and inevitability of hard, deductive logic.

> *We also rejoice in our sufferings, because we know that suffering produces perseverance; perseverance, character; and character, hope. And hope does not disappoint us.*

A word can also be repeated, but with a change of meaning, either a subtle, ambiguous change (ploce) or a more obvious grammatical change (polyptoton). Ploce emphasizes a contrast by playing on ambiguity, while polyptoton suggests both a connection and a difference. In the following line, 'Love is not love' is an example of ploce, while 'alter' and 'alteration' and 'remover' and 'remove' are examples of polyptoton.

> *Love is not love which alters when it alteration finds,*
> *Or bends with the remover to remove.*

As well as single words, groups of words can be repeated, either at the beginning of successive clauses or lines (anaphora), or at the end of successive clauses or lines (epistrophe/epiphora).

> *I fled Him, down the nights and down the days;*
> *I fled Him, down the arches of the years;*
> *I fled Him, down the labyrinthine ways*
> *Of my own mind...*

> *There is no Negro problem. There is no Southern problem. There is no Northern problem. There is only an American problem.*

If you want to throw the kitchen sink at it, you can combine anaphora with epistrophe (symploce).

> *When there is talk of hatred, let us stand up and talk against it. When there is talk of violence, let us stand up and talk against it.*

In this particular example, the repetition conveys determination, resolve, and togetherness.

3. Idea or structure repetition

The repetition of an idea or structure can, if used correctly, add richness and resonance to expression. It can also add emphasis; create order, rhythm, and progression; and conjure up a total concept.

Let's start with tautology, which is the repetition of the same idea within a line.

> *With malice toward none, with charity for all.*

Pleonasm is a type of tautology entailing the use of more words than is necessary for clear expression.

> *I am the Alpha and the Omega, the First and the Last, the Beginning and the End.*

The latter example is a combination of pleonasm and parallelism, which involves using a similar syntactical structure in a pair or series of related words, clauses, or lines. Three parallel words, clauses, or lines constitutes a tricolon, which is a particularly effective type of isocolon.

> *Mad, bad, and dangerous to know*

Structural or syntactical parallels can be highlighted by means of structural reversal (chiasmus).

> *But many that are first shall be last; and the last shall be first.*

> *Give not that which is holy unto the dogs, neither cast ye your pearls before swine, lest they* [the swine] *trample them under their feet, and* [the dogs] *turn again and rend you.*

4. Unusual structure

An unusual structure draws attention and can also create a shift in emphasis.

Hyperbaton is the alteration of the normal order of the words in a sentence, or the separation of words that normally go together. There are several types. Anastrophe involves inversion of ordinary word order. Hypallage involves transference of attributes from their proper subjects to others. Hysteron proteron involves inversion of natural chronology.

> *Above the seas to stand* (anastrophe)

> *Angry crown of kings* (hypallage)

> *Let us die, and charge into the thick of the fight.* (hysteron proteron)

Zeugma is the joining of two or more parts of a sentence with a single verb (or sometimes a noun). Depending upon the position of the verb (at the beginning, in the middle, or at the end), a zeugma is either a prozeugma, mesozeugma, or hypozeugma. Here is an example of a mesozeugma:

> *What a shame is this, that neither hope of reward, nor feare of reproach could any thing move him, neither the persuasion of his friends, nor the love of his country.*

Syllepsis is a type of zeugma in which a single word agrees grammatically with two or more other words, but semantically with only one.

> *She lowered her standards by raising her glass, her courage, her eyes, and his hopes.*

Hypozeuxis is the reverse of zeugma, wherein each subject is attached to its own verb. The following, from Churchill, is also an example of anaphora (see above):

> *We shall fight on the beaches. We shall fight on the landing grounds. We shall fight in the fields, and in the streets, we shall fight in the hills. We shall never surrender!*

A periodic sentence is one that is not grammatically or semantically complete before the final clause.

> *Every breath you take, every move you make, every bond you break, every step you take, I'll be watching you.*

5. Language games

Language games such as puns and deliberate mistakes can draw attention to a phrase or idea, or simply raise a smile, by creating new and often ridiculous images and associations. They can also give rise to a vivid image, create ambiguity, and suggest sincerity and even passion.

A pun (or paronomasia) is a play on words that sound alike, or on a word that has more than one meaning.

> *Do hotel managers get board with their jobs?*

> *A dog gave birth to puppies near the road and was cited for littering.*

> *She is nice from far, but far from nice.*

Catachresis is the intentional misuse of a word or turn of phrase, for example, using one word for another, or straining or mixing metaphors.

> *To take arms against a sea of troubles...*

> *'Tis deepest winter in Lord Timon's purse*

Antitimeria is the intentional misuse of a word as if it were a member of a different word class, typically a noun for a verb.

> *I'll unhair thy head.*

Enallage is the intentional and effective use of incorrect grammar.

> *Let him kiss me with the kisses of his mouth, for thy love is better than wine.*

> *Love me tender, love me true*

6. Opposition and contradiction

The use of opposition or contradiction draws attention to itself, forces thought, can be humorous, and can suggest progression and completion.

An oxymoron is a juxtaposition of words which at first sight seems contradictory or incongruous. A paradox is similar to an oxymoron, but less compact.

> *Make haste slowly*

> *What a pity that youth must be wasted on the young.*

Antiphrasis is the use of a word in a context in which it means its opposite.

> *A giant of five foot three inches*

Antithesis is the use of a pair of opposites for contrasting effect. A series of antitheses is called a progression.

A time to be born, and a time to die; a time to plant, and a time to pluck up that which is planted; a time to kill, and a time to heal...

7. Circumlocution

Circumlocution works by painting a picture, or conjuring up a complex idea, with just a few well-chosen words.

Hendiadys is the juxtaposition of two words, and hendriatris of three.

Dieu et mon droit

Sex, drugs, and rock'n'roll

Lock, stock, and barrel

The last example is also a merism, which involves enumerating the parts to signify the whole. Here's another merism:

For better for worse, for richer for poorer, in sickness and in health...

8. Imagery

Obviously, imagery works by conjuring up a particular image.

Metonymy is the naming of a thing or concept by another thing that is closely associated with it.

> *Downing Street*

> *The pen is mightier than the sword*

Antonomasia, a type of metonymy, is the use of a word or phrase or epithet in place of a proper name.

> *The Divine Teacher* (Plato)

> *The Master of Those Who Know* (Aristotle)

> *The Subtle Doctor* (Duns Scotus)

Synedoche, which is similar to metonymy, is the naming of a thing or concept by one of its parts.

> *A pair of hands*

> *Longshanks*

With rhetoric, it is not the logic but the beauty and eloquence and vividness that does the persuading.

In Plato's *Lysis*, Socrates says that beauty 'is certainly a soft, smooth, slippery thing, and therefore of a nature which easily slips in and permeates our souls'.

You will, of course, have noticed the sensual sibilance of that phrase.

7

Language

Time heaved a gentle sigh as the wind swept through the willows. Communication does not require language, and many animals communicate effectively by other means and modes. However, language is closely associated with symbolism, and so with conceptual thought and creativity. These unique assets make us by far the most adaptable of all animals and enable us to engage in highly abstract pursuits such as art, science, and philosophy that define us as human beings.

Here's a thought experiment. Imagine what it would be like to live without language—not without the ability to speak, but without an actual language. Given the choice, would you rather lose the faculty of sight or the faculty of language? This is probably the first time that you have been faced with this question: the faculty of language is so fundamental to the human condition that, unlike the faculty of sight, we take it completed for granted. 'Monkeys' quipped Kenneth Grahame 'very sensibly refrain from speech, lest they should be set to earn their livings.'

If rhetoric, the beauty of language, can so bend us (Chapter 6), how about language itself? In other words, how does the language you speak influence the way you think?

The ostensible purpose of language is to transmit thoughts from one mind to another. Language represents thought, that's for sure, but does it also determine thought?

Wittgenstein famously wrote that 'the limits of my language stand for the limits of my world'. Taken at face value, that seems too strong a claim. There are over 7,000 languages in the world—with, by some estimates, one dying out every two weeks or so. The number of basic colour terms varies quite considerably from one language to another. Dani, spoken in New Guinea, and Bassa, spoken in Liberia and Sierra Leone, each have no more than two colour terms, one for dark/cool colours and the other for light/warm colours. But, obviously, speakers of Dani and Bassa are able to perceive and think about more than just two colours.

More subtly, there is no English equivalent for the German word *Sehnsucht*, which denotes dissatisfaction with reality and yearning for a richer, 'realer' ideal. But despite lacking the word, Walt Whitman was clearly able to conjure up both the concept and the emotion:

> *Is it a dream?*
> *Nay, but the lack of it the dream,*
> *And, failing it, life's lore and wealth a dream,*
> *And all the world a dream.*

Language

Figure 3: Silence is the language of God, all else is poor translation. —Rumi

The English language has a word for children who have lost their parents (orphan), and a word for spouses who have lost their spouse (widow or widower), but no word for parents who have lost a child. This may mean that parents who have lost a child are less likely to enter our minds, but not that they cannot enter our minds or that we cannot conceive of them. We often think about or remember things that cannot be put into words, such as the smell and taste of a mango, the dawn chorus of the birds, or the contours of a lover's face or other part of their anatomy. Animals and pre-linguistic babies must surely have thoughts, even though they have no language.

If language does not determine thought, how, if at all, does it interact with thought? Russian, Greek, and many other languages have two words for blue, one for lighter shades and the other for darker shades—*goluboy* and *siniy* in Russian, and *ghalazio* and *ble* in Greek. A study found that, compared to English speakers, Russian speakers were quicker to discriminate between shades of *goluboy* and *siniy*, but not between shades of *goluboy* or shades of *siniy*. Conversely, another study found that Greek speakers who had lived in the UK for a long time see *ghalazio* and *ble* as more similar than Greek speakers living in Greece. By creating categories, by carving up the world, language enhances cognition.

In contrast to modern Greek, Ancient Greek, in common with many ancient languages, has no specific word for blue, leaving Homer to speak of 'the wine-dark sea'. But the Ancient Greeks did have several words for love, including *philia*, *eros*, *storge*, and *agape*, each one referring to a different type or concept of love, respectively, friendship, sexual love, familial love, and universal love. This means that the Ancient Greeks could speak more precisely about love, but does it also mean that they could think more precisely about love, and, as a result, have more fulfilled love lives? Or perhaps they had more words for love because they had more fulfilled love lives in the first place, or, more prosaically, because their culture and society placed more emphasis on the different bonds that can exist between people, and on the various duties and expectations that attend, or attended, to those bonds.

Philosophers and academics sometimes make up words to help them talk and think about an issue. In the *Phaedrus*, Plato coined the word *psychagogia*, the art of leading souls, to characterize *rhetoric*—another word that he invented. Every field of human endeavour invariably evolves its own specialized jargon. There seems to be an important relationship between language and thought: I often speak—or write, as I am doing right now—to define or refine my thinking on a particular topic, and language is the scaffolding by which I arrive at my more subtle or syncretic thoughts.

While we're talking dead languages, it may come as a surprise that Latin has no direct translations for 'yes' and 'no'. Instead, one either echoes the verb in the question (in affirmative or negative) or expresses one's feelings about the truth value of the proposition with adverbs such as *certe, fortasse, nimirum, plane, vero, etiam, sane, minime*... This may have led to more nuanced thinking, as well as greater interpersonal engagement, though it must have been a nightmare for teens.

Much of the particularity of a language is extra-lexical, built into the syntax and grammar of the language and virtually invisible to native speakers. English, for example, restricts the use of the present perfect tense ('has been', 'has read') to subjects who are still alive, marking a sharp grammatical divide between the living and the dead, and, by extension, between life and death. But of course, as an English speaker, you already knew that, at least subconsciously. Language is full of built-in assumptions and prejudices.

Here's another, more substantial example: When describing accidental events, English speakers tend to emphasize the agent ('I fired the gun') more than, say, speakers of Spanish or Japanese, who prefer to omit the agent ('the gun went off').

One study found that, as a result, English speakers are more likely to remember the agents of accidental events—and, I surmise, to attach blame.

Some languages seem more egocentric than others. Many languages forgo the explicit use of the personal pronoun, which is instead built into the verb. For example, 'I want' in Spanish is simply *quiero*. English in contrast requires the explicit use of the personal pronoun in all cases. As does French. What's more, French speakers often redouble on the personal pronoun, as in *Moi, je pense que...* ['Me, I think that'] with the stress on the *moi*. Sometimes, they also redouble on other personal pronouns, *Et toi, qu'en penses-tu?* ['And you, what do you think about it?']. But redoubling on the first personal pronoun is much more common: *Bon aller, moi j'en ai marre hein* ['Whatever, I'm fed up me']. This redoubling is more a feature of the spoken than the written word, and, depending on context, can serve to emphasize or simply acknowledge a difference of opinion. Equivalent forms in English are more strained and recondite, and less often used, for example, 'Well, as for me, I think that...' The redoubling, in French, on the first-person personal pronoun seems to inject drama into a conversation, as though the speaker were acting out her own part, or playing up her difference and separateness.

In English, verbs express tense, that is, time relative to the moment of speaking. In Turkish, they also express the source of the information (evidentiality)—whether the information is direct, acquired through sense perception; or indirect, acquired by testimony or inference. In Russian, verbs include information about completion, with (to simplify) the perfective aspect used for completed actions and the imperfective aspect for ongoing or habitual actions. Spanish, on the other hand, emphasizes modes of being, with two verbs for 'to be'—*ser*, to indicate permanent or lasting attributes, and *estar*, to indicate temporary states and locations. Like many languages, Spanish has more than one mode of second-person address: *tú* for intimates and social inferiors, and *usted* for strangers and social superiors, equivalent to *tu* and *vous* in French, and *tu* and *lei* in Italian. There used to be a similar distinction in English, with 'thou' used to express intimacy, familiarity, or downright rudeness—but because it is archaic, many people now think of it as more formal than 'you'. It stands to reason that, compared to English speakers, Turkish speakers have to pay more attention to evidentiality, Russian speakers to completion, and Spanish speakers to modes of being and social relations.

In many languages, nouns are divided into masculine and feminine. In German, there is a third, neutral class of nouns. In Dyribal, an Aboriginal language, there are four noun classes, including one for women, water, fire, violence, and exceptional animals—or, as George Lakoff put it, 'women, fire, and dangerous things'. Researchers asked speakers of German and Spanish to describe objects with opposite gender assignments in these two languages and found that their descriptions conformed to gender stereotypes, even when the testing took place in English. For example, German speakers described bridges (feminine in German, *die Brücke*) as beautiful, elegant, fragile, peaceful, pretty, and slender, whereas Spanish speakers described bridges (masculine in Spanish, *el puente*) as big, dangerous, long, strong, sturdy, and towering.

Another study looking at the artistic personification of abstract concepts such as love, justice, and time found that, in 78% of cases, the gender of the concept in the artist's language predicted the gender of the personification, and that this pattern held even for uncommon allegories such as geometry, necessity, and silence. Compared to a French or Spanish artist, a German artist is far more likely to paint death [*der Tod, la mort, la muerte*] or victory [*der Sieg, la Victoire, la Victoria*] as a man—though all artists, or at least all European artists, tend to paint death in skeletal form. Grammar, it seems, can directly and radically influence thought, perception, and action.

It is often said that, by de-emphasizing them, language perpetuates biases against women. For example, many writers in English continue to use 'mankind' to talk about humankind, and 'he' for 'he or she'. Similarly, many languages use masculine plural pronouns to refer to groups of people with at least one man. If a hundred women turn up with a baby in a pram, and that baby happens to be male, French grammar dictates the use of the masculine plural *ils*: *ils sont arrivés*, 'they have arrived'.

Language changes as attitudes change, and sometimes politicians, pressure groups, and others attempt to change the language to change the attitudes—but, on the whole, language, or at least grammar, serves to preserve the status quo, to crystallize the order and culture that it reflects.

Language is also made up of all sorts of metaphors. In English and Swedish, people tend to speak of time in terms of distance: 'I won't be long'; 'let's look at the weather for the week ahead'; 'his drinking finally caught up with him'. But in Spanish or Greek, people tend to speak of time in terms of size or volume—for example, in Spanish, *hacemos una pequeña pausa* ['let's have a small break'] rather than *corta pausa* ['short break']. More generally, *mucho tiempo* ['much time'] is preferred to *largo tiempo* ['long time'], and, in Greek, *poli ora* to *makry kroniko diastima*. And guess what? According to a recent study of fully bilingual Spanish-Swedish speakers, the language used to estimate the duration of events alters the speaker's perception of the relative passage of time.

But all in all, with perhaps a couple of exceptions, European languages do not differ dramatically from one another. To talk about space, speakers of Kuuk Thaayorre, an Aboriginal language, use 16 words for absolute cardinal directions instead of relative references such as 'right in front of you', 'to the right', and 'over there'. As a result, even children are always aware of the exact direction in which they are facing. When asked to arrange a sequence of picture cards in temporal order, English speakers arrange the cards from left to right, whereas Hebrew speakers tend to arrange them from right to left. But speakers of Kuuk Thaayorre consistently arrange them from east to west, which is left to right if they are facing south, and right to left if they are facing north. Thinking differently about space, they seem to think differently about time as well.

Language may not determine thought, but it focuses perception and attention on particular aspects of reality, structures and enhances cognitive processes, and even to some extent regulates social relationships. Our language reflects and at the same time shapes our thoughts and, ultimately, our culture, which in turn shapes our thoughts and language. There is no equivalent in English of the Portuguese word *saudade*, which refers to the love and longing for someone or something that has been lost and may never be regained. The rise of *saudade* coincided with the decline of Portugal and the yen for its imperial heyday, a yen so strong as to have written itself into the national anthem: *Levantai hoje de novo o esplendor de Portugal* ['Let us once again lift up the splendour of Portugal']. The three threads of language, thought, and culture are so tightly woven that they cannot be prised apart.

It has been said that when an old man dies, a library burns to the ground. But when a language dies, it is a whole world that comes to an end.

8
Languages

If the language you speak influences the way you think, what happens when you learn another language?

It can come as a surprise to many people in the UK and US that speaking more than one language is the norm rather than the exception. In prehistoric times, most people belonged to small linguistic communities, and spoke several languages to trade with, and marry into, neighbouring communities.

Still today, remaining populations of hunter-gatherers are nearly all multilingual. Papua New Guinea, a country smaller than Spain, counts some 850 languages, or about one language per 10,000 inhabitants. In countries such as India, Malaysia, and South Africa, most people are bilingual or better. Even in the world at large, polyglots outnumber monoglots. And with the advent of the Internet, contact with foreign languages has become increasingly frequent, even for the most linguistically isolated of monoglots.

In sixteenth century England, Queen Elizabeth I could speak at least nine languages: English, French, Spanish, Italian, Latin, Welsh, Cornish, Scottish, and Irish. A few days after her death in 1603, the Venetian ambassador Giovanni Carlo Scaramelli wrote back to his Doge and Senate:

> She possessed nine languages so thoroughly that each appeared to be her native tongue; five of these were the languages of peoples governed by her, English, Welsh, Cornish, Scottish, for that part of her possessions where they are still savage, and Irish. All of them are so different, that it is impossible for those who speak the one to understand any of the others. Besides this, she spoke perfectly Latin, French, Spanish, and Italian extremely well.

No wonder she didn't want to get married.

To speak a language competently implies knowledge of the culture associated with the language. Multilingualism is closely linked to multiculturalism, and, historically, both came under attack with the rise of the nation state. In the aftermath of the 2016 Brexit referendum, the British Prime Minister Theresa May stated: 'If you believe you are a citizen of the world, you are a citizen of nowhere'—as though that were somehow deviant or problematic. Human beings are far older than any nation. Still today, some people believe that teaching a child more than one language can impair the child's linguistic and cognitive development. But what's the evidence?

According to several studies, people who learn another language do significantly better on standardized tests. Language management calls upon executive functions such as attention control, cognitive inhibition, and working memory, and there is mounting evidence that bi- and multi-lingual people are better at analysing their surroundings, multitasking, and problem solving. They also have a larger working memory, including for tasks that do not involve language. In terms of brain structure, they have more grey matter (and associated activity) in the dorsal anterior cingulate cortex, a locus for language control and broader executive function. Superior executive function is, in turn, a strong predictor of academic success.

Being multilingual can also improve your judgement. According to one recent study, people who think through a moral dilemma in a foreign language make much more rational, or utilitarian, decisions, perhaps because certain words lose some of their emotional weight, or because the problem is seen from a different cultural perspective or processed through different neural channels. So, if you have a second language, you can use it, like a good friend, to check yourself.

The cognitive benefits of bi- and multilingualism, disputed though they are, seem to yield important health dividends. An examination of hospital records in Toronto uncovered that bilingual patients were diagnosed with dementia on average three to four years later than their monolingual counterparts, despite being of a similar educational and occupational status. A more recent study in Northern Italy looking at patients at the same stage of Alzheimer's disease revealed that the bilingual patients were on average five years older, and that they had stronger connections between the brain areas involved in executive function. Similarly, research into 600 stroke survivors in India found that the bilingual patients had a much better outcome: specifically, 40.5% of the bilingual patients had normal cognition compared to just 19.6% of the monolingual ones.

And then there are the undisputed economic benefits. A US study found that high-level bilingualism is associated with extra earnings of about $3,000 a year, even after controlling for factors such as educational attainment and parental socio-economic status. According to *The Economist*, for an American graduate, a second language could be worth—on a conservative estimate—up to $128,000 over forty years. Of course, the overall economic impact of multilingualism is much greater than the sum of the higher earnings of multilingual speakers. A report from the University of Geneva estimates that Switzerland's multilingual heritage contributes about $50 billion a year to the Swiss economy, or as much as 10% of GDP. In contrast, research for the UK government cautions that a lack of language skills could be costing the British economy around $48 billion a year, or 3.5% of GDP, in lost output.

Being bilingual may have important cognitive and economic benefits, but it is usually the personal, social, and cultural benefits that multilingual people are most keen to emphasize. Many bilingual people feel that the way they are, and the way they see the world—and even the way they laugh and love—changes according to the language that they are speaking. In the 1960s, Susan Ervin-Tripp asked Japanese-English bilingual women to finish sentences in each language, and found that the women came up with very different endings depending on whether they were speaking English or Japanese. For example, they completed 'Real friends should…' with '…help each other' in Japanese, but '…be frank' in English. 'Who's your favourite writer?' 'What do you want to eat for dinner?' Ask a question in one language, and you get one answer; ask the same question in another language, and you might get a different one. 'To have another language' said Charlemagne 'is to have another soul'.

Translation dictionaries seem to assume that languages are made up of corresponding words, but even when that is more or less the case, the equivalencies have different connotations. Compared to 'I like you' in English, *je t'aime* in French is a far more serious proposition. George Carlin once joked that 'meow' means 'woof' in cat—but, of course, it doesn't. Owing to a certain *je ne sais quoi*, some things are more readily expressed in one language than in another. By code switching, multilingual speakers can increase their range of expression and perhaps even their range of thought. In the words of Wittgenstein: 'A picture held us captive. And we could not get outside it, for it lay in our language and language seemed to repeat it to us inexorably.'

Certain languages are better suited to certain purposes, for example, English is great for science and technology, French is better for cooking and whispering, and Latin is best for praying and formal rites of passage. Multilingual people are free to pick and choose, maybe along the lines of Charles V, Holy Roman Emperor: 'I speak in Latin to God, Italian to Women, French to Men, and German to my Horse.' Charles V did not get on with the German lords and preferred to live in Spain, sitting on the newly created Spanish throne by right of his incarcerated mother, Joanna the Mad—things I know because I speak Spanish.

The more languages you learn, the easier it becomes to learn languages. But learning a language also strengthens your first language. For instance, one study found that Spanish immersion significantly improved children's native English vocabulary. More broadly, learning a language casts light upon your first language and language in general, increasing your appreciation of language and ability to communicate. 'You speak English beautifully,' wrote Robert Aickman in *The Wine-Dark Sea*, 'which means you can't be English.'

While writing this chapter, I asked my amazing Facebook and Twitter people the following question: 'if you are bi- or multilingual, what do you most value about that fact?'

And here are some of their responses:

- The freedom to access different cultures plus the possibility to read many authors in original version!
- Being fluent in a couple of other languages has given me insight into other ways of seeing the world. That helps empathy, and openness.
- I appreciate the cognitive advantages being multilingual has offered. Also the connections with culture, history, and the knowledge acquired.
- Language is knowledge. Always useful to be a little less ignorant.

- It feels as if I can switch into two different modes and think from different perspectives.
- Being more tolerant—new language = new culture, new and different perspectives/access to more information.
- That I can talk wine with twice as many ppl.
- It gives me patience and understanding for those who want to articulate, but have difficulty conveying what they really mean.
- The fact that I can fully understand and communicate in another language (Afrikaans) makes me feel good.
- It gave me an understanding that 'thoughts' don't come into my head in a language at all. Thoughts come as 'ideas'. Only when I have to verbalize my ideas, I have to use a language.
- I'm bilingual in India. There's nothing special about it here. Know a ton of people who are trilingual. In India, multilingualism starts becoming impressive if the language count's above like five or something.
- Obviously, being able to speak about people in elevators without them knowing what's said. ;-)
- Having a variety of options when cussing.

Every language has its own rules and conventions, its own sounds and rhythms, its own beauty and poetry, its own history and philosophy.

Every language is another way of being human, another way of being alive.

9

Reason

For Aristotle, our unique capacity to reason is what defines us as human beings. Therefore, our happiness, or our flourishing, consists in leading a life that enables us to use and develop our reason, and that is in accordance with reason.

Article 1 of the Universal Declaration of Human Rights (1948) states that all human beings are 'endowed with reason', and it has long been held that reason is something that God gave us, that we share with God, and that is the divine, immortal element within us. As per John 1:1: In the beginning was the Word [Greek, *logos*, 'word', 'reason'], and the Word was with God, and the Word was God.

[In passing, isn't it interesting, especially in our context, that Greek has the same word, *logos*, for both 'word' and 'reason'? In fact, Aristotle used *logos* specifically to mean 'reasoned discourse'. *Logos* derives from the Proto Indo-European root *leg-*, 'to collect, gather', and is related to many English words including: intelligence (the subject of the next chapter), apology, colleague, college, delegate, lecture, legal, legend, logic, and privilege. In the *Cratylus*, the first and most charming treatise on the philosophy of language, Plato says that 'the knowledge of names is a great part of knowledge'.]

At the dawn of the so-called Age of Reason, Descartes doubted everything except his ability to reason. 'Because reason' he wrote, 'is the only thing that makes us men, and distinguishes us from the beasts, I would prefer to believe that it exists, in its entirety, in each of us...'

But what exactly is reason? Reason, for a start, is more than mere associative thinking, more than the mere ability to move from one idea (such as storm clouds) to another (such as imminent rain). Associative thinking can result from processes other than reason, such as instinct, learning, or intuition (Chapter 15). Reason, in contrast, involves providing reasons—ideally good reasons—for an association. And it involves using a system of representation, such as thought or language, to derive or arrive at that association.

People often amalgamate reason with logic, especially formal, deductive logic (Chapter 1). At the very least, formal logic is seen as the purest form of reason. True, formal logic is basically an attempt to codify the most reliable or fail-safe forms of reasoning. But it is concerned merely with the validity of arguments, with the right relationship between premises and conclusion. It is not concerned with the actual truth or falsity of the premises or, indeed, the merit or relevance of the conclusion.

Reason in contrast is a much broader psychological activity which also involves selecting and assessing evidence, creating and testing hypotheses, weighing competing arguments, evaluating means and ends, developing and applying heuristics (mental shortcuts), and so on. All this, as you may have experienced in Chapters 3 and 4, requires the use of judgement, which is why reason, unlike logic, cannot be delegated to a computer, and also why it so often fails to persuade. Logic is but a tool of reason, and it can sometimes be reasonable to accept something that is or appears to be illogical.

It is often thought, not least in educational establishments, that 'logic' is able to provide immediate certainty and the authority or credibility that goes with it. But logic is a lot more limited than many people imagine. Logic essentially consists in a set of operations for deriving a statement from other statements. In a sense, it merely makes explicit that which was previously implicit. It brings nothing new to the table. The conclusion merely flows from the premises as their inevitable consequence:

> *All birds have feathers. (Premise 1)*
> *Woodpeckers are birds. (Premise 2)*
> *Therefore, woodpeckers have feathers. (Conclusion)*

Another major problem with logic is that it relies on premises that are founded, not on logic itself, but on inductive reasoning. How do we know that 'all birds have feathers'? Well, we don't know for sure. We merely suppose that they do because, so far, every bird that we have seen or heard about has had feathers. But the existence of birds without feathers, if only in the fossil record, is not beyond the bounds of possibility. Many avian species are hatched naked, and a featherless bird called Rhea recently took the Internet by storm. A lot also depends on how and how tightly we define our terms, especially, in this case, 'bird'. There are in fact several definitions of what a bird might be, including, for example, 'all archosaurs closer to birds than to crocodiles' and 'advanced archosaurs with feathers'...

Inductive reasoning only ever yields probabilistic 'truths', and yet it is the basis of everything that we know or think that we know about the world we live in. Our only justification for induction is that it has worked in the past, which is, of course, an inductive proof, tantamount to saying that induction works because induction works! To rescue it from this Problem of Induction, Karl Popper argued that science proceeds not inductively but deductively, by making bold claims and then seeking to falsify those claims. But if Popper is right, science could never tell us what is, but only ever what is not. I shall return to Popper and the Problem of Induction in Chapter 13 on science.

Putting these inductive/deductive worries aside, reason is limited in reach, if not in theory then at least in practice. The movement of a simple pendulum is regular and easy to predict, but the movement of a double pendulum (a pendulum with another pendulum attached to its end) is extremely chaotic. If you're interested, there are videos of double pendula on the Internet. Similarly, the interaction between two physical bodies such as the sun and the earth can be reduced to a simple formula, but the interaction between three physical bodies is much more complex—which is why the length of the lunar month is not a constant and the length of any one lunar month is extremely difficult to approximate. But even Three-Body Problems are as nothing compared to the entanglement of human affairs. God, it is sometimes said, gave all the easy problems to the physicists.

The intricacies of human affairs often lead to a paralysis of reason, and we are left confused and undecided, sometimes for years and even into the grave. To cut through all this complexity, we rely heavily on forces such as emotions and desires—which is why Aristotle's *Rhetoric* on the art of arguing includes a detailed dissection of what used to be called the passions. Our emotions and desires define the aims or goals of our reasoning. They determine the parameters of any particular deliberation and carry to conscious attention only a small selection of all the available facts and counterfactuals. Brain injured people with a diminished capacity for emotion find it especially hard to make decisions, as do people with apathy, which is a symptom of severe depression and other mental disorders. Relying so heavily on the emotions comes at a cost, which is, of course, that emotions aren't rational, and, more than that, can distort reasoning. Fear alone can open the gate on all manner of self-deception (Chapter 5). On the other hand, that emotions aren't rational need not make them irrational. As I argued in a book called *Heaven and Hell: The Psychology of the Emotions*, some emotions are appropriate or justified while others are not. This is why, as well as coming to grips with maths and science, it is so important to educate our emotions. I'll be delving more deeply into the emotions in Chapter 19.

Another shortcoming of reason is that it sometimes leads to conclusions that seem unreasonable, or even contradicts itself. In *On Generation and Corruption*, Aristotle says that, while the arguments of certain thinkers may appear to follow logically in dialectical discussion, 'to believe them seems next door to madness when one considers the facts'. In Plato's *Lesser Hippias*, Socrates manages to argue that people who commit injustice voluntarily are better than those who do so involuntarily, but then confesses that he sometimes thinks the opposite, and sometimes goes back and forth:

> *My present state of mind is due to our previous argument, which inclines me to believe that in general those who do wrong involuntarily are worse than those who do wrong voluntarily, and therefore I hope that you will be good to me, and not refuse to heal me; for you will do me a much greater benefit if you cure my soul of ignorance, than you would if you were to cure my body of disease.*

The sophists of Classical Greece taught rhetoric to wealthy young men with ambitions of holding public office. Prominent sophists included Protagoras, Gorgias, Prodicus, Hippias, Thrasymachus, Callicles, and Euthydemus, all of whom feature as characters in Plato's dialogues. Protagoras charged extortionate fees for his services. He once took on a pupil, Euathlus, on the understanding that he would be paid once Euathlus had won his first court case. However, Euathlus never won a case, and eventually Protagoras sued him for non-payment. Protagoras argued that if he won the case he would be paid, and if Euathlus won the case, he still would be paid, because Euathlus would have won a case. Euathlus, having picked up a trick or two from his master, retorted that if he won the case he would not have to pay, and if Protagoras won the case, he still would not have to pay, because he still would not have won a case!

Whereas philosophers such as Plato and Socrates use reason to arrive at the truth, sophists such as Protagoras abuse reason to move mobs and enrich themselves. But we are after all social animals, and reason evolved more as a means of solving practical problems and influencing people than as a ladder to abstract truths. What's more, reason is not a solitary but a collective enterprise: premises are at least partially (and often entirely) reliant on the achievements of others, and we ourselves make much better progress when prompted and challenged by our peers.

The principal theme of Plato's *Protagoras* is the teachability of virtue. At the end of the dialogue, Socrates remarks that he began by arguing that virtue cannot be taught, only to end by arguing that virtue is no other than knowledge, and therefore that it can be taught. Protagoras, in contrast, began by arguing that virtue can be taught, but ended by arguing that some forms of virtue are not knowledge, and therefore cannot be taught! Had they not debated, both men would have stuck with their original, crude opinions and been no better off.

Why does reason say ridiculous things and contradict itself? Perhaps the biggest problem is with that old chestnut, language. Words and sentences can be vague or ambiguous.

If you remove a single grain from a heap of sand, it is still a heap of sand. But what happens if you keep on repeating the process? Is a single extant grain still a heap? If not, at what point did the heap pass from being a heap to a non-heap? When the wine critic Jancis Robinson asked on Twitter what qualifies someone to call themselves a sommelier, she received at least a dozen different responses. Similarly, we might say to someone something like, 'You can't do that. Well, you can, but...'

Another big problem is with the way we are. Our senses are crude and limited. More subtly, our minds come with built-in notions that may have served our species well but do not accurately or even approximately reflect reality. Zeno's paradoxes, for example, flush out the limits of our understanding of something as rudimentary as movement. Some of Zeno's paradoxes side with quantum theory in suggesting that space and time are discrete, while others side with the theory of relativity in suggesting that they are continuous. As far as I know (I'm not a physicist), quantum theory and the theory of relativity remain completely unreconciled. Other concepts, such as infinity or what lies outside the universe, are simply beyond our ability to conceive.

A final sticking point is with self-referential statements, such as 'This statement is false'. If the statement is false, it is true; but if it is true, it is not false. But let's not open that can of worms.

Despite its shortcomings, I hold reason in the highest regard. It is after all the foundation of our peace and freedom, which are under constant threat from the blind forces of unreason. In highlighting the limits of reason as I have just done, I seek not to disparage or undermine it but to understand and use it better, and even to revel in it.

'The last function of reason', said Blaise Pascal, 'is to recognize that there are an infinity of things which are beyond it. It is but feeble if it does not see so far as to know this.'

Figure 4: The Sleep of Reason Produces Monsters. Francisco José de Goya y Lucientes.

10

Intelligence

There is no agreed definition or model of intelligence. By the Collins English Dictionary, intelligence is 'the ability to think, reason, and understand instead of doing things automatically or by instinct'. By the Macmillan Dictionary, it is 'the ability to understand and think about things, and to gain and use knowledge'.

In seeking to define intelligence, a good place to start might be with dementia. In Alzheimer's disease, the most common form of dementia, there is disturbance of multiple higher cortical functions including memory, thinking, orientation, comprehension, calculation, learning capacity, language, and judgement. I think it significant that people with dementia or severe learning difficulties cope very poorly with changes to their environment, such as moving into a care home or even into an adjacent room. Taken together, this suggests that, at its broadest, intelligence refers to the functioning of a number of related faculties and abilities that enable us to respond to environmental pressures. Because this is not beyond animals and even plants, they too can be said to be possessed of intelligence.

We Westerners tend to think of intelligence in terms of analytical skills. But in a close-knit hunter-gatherer society, intelligence might be defined more in terms of foraging skills or social skills and responsibilities. Even within a single society, the skills that are most valued change over time. In the West, the emphasis has gradually shifted from language skills to more purely analytical skills, and it is only in 1960, well within living memory, that the Universities of Oxford and Cambridge dropped Latin as an entry requirement. In 1990, Peter Salovey and John Mayer published the seminal paper on emotional intelligence, and EI quickly became all the rage. In that same year, Tim Berners-Lee wrote the first web browser. Today, we cannot go very far without having some considerable IT skills (certainly by the standards of 1990), and computer scientists are among some of the most highly paid professionals. Therefore, what constitutes intelligence varies according to our priorities and values.

Contemporary society holds analytical skills in such high regard that some of our political leaders cite their 'high IQ' to defend their more egregious actions. This Western emphasis on reason and intelligence has its roots in Ancient Greece with Socrates, his pupil Plato, and Plato's pupil Aristotle. Socrates held that 'the unexamined life is not worth living'. He typically taught by the dialectic or Socratic method, that is, by questioning one or more people about a particular concept such as courage or justice so as to expose a contradiction in their initial assumptions and provoke a reappraisal of the concept. For Plato, reason could carry us far beyond the confines of common sense and everyday experience into a 'hyper-heaven' [Greek, *hyperouranos*] of ideal forms. He famously fantasized about putting a geniocracy of philosopher kings in charge of his utopic Republic. Finally, Aristotle argued that our distinctive function as human beings is our unique capacity to reason, and therefore that our supreme good and happiness consists in leading a life of rational contemplation (Chapter 9). To paraphrase Aristotle in Book X of the *Nicomachean Ethics,* 'man more than anything is reason, and the life of reason is the most self-sufficient, the most pleasant, the happiest, the best, and the most divine of all.' In later centuries, reason became a divine property, found in man because made in God's image. If you struggled with your SATs, or thought they were pants, you now know who to blame.

Unfortunately, the West's obsession with analytical intelligence has had, and continues to have, dire moral, political, and social consequences. Immanuel Kant most memorably made the connection between reasoning and moral standing, arguing (in simple terms) that, by virtue of their ability to reason, human beings ought to be treated, not as means to an end, but as ends-in-themselves. From here, it becomes all too easy to conclude that, the better you are at reasoning, the worthier you are of personhood and its rights and privileges. For centuries, women were deemed to be 'emotional', that is, less rational, which justified treating them as chattel or, at best, second-class citizens. The same could be said of non-white people, over whom it was not just the right but the duty of the white man to rule. Rudyard Kipling's poem *The White Man's Burden* (1902) begins with the lines:

Take up the White Man's burden–
Send forth the best ye breed–
Go bind your sons to exile
To serve your captives' need;
To wait in heavy harness
On fluttered folk and wild–
Your new-caught, sullen peoples,
Half-devil and half-child.

People deemed to be less rational—women, non-white people, the lower classes, the infirm, the 'deviant'—were not just disenfranchised but dominated, colonized, enslaved, murdered, and sterilized, in all impunity. Only in 2015 did the US Senate vote to compensate living victims of government-sponsored sterilization programmes for the, I quote, 'feeble-minded'. Today, of all people, it is the white man who most fears artificial intelligence, imagining that it will usurp his status and privilege.

According to one recent paper, IQ is the best predictor of job performance. But that is not altogether surprising given that 'performance' and IQ have been defined in similar terms, and that both depend, at least to some extent, on third factors such as compliance, motivation, and educational attainment.

Genius in contrast is more a matter of drive, vision, creativity, and luck or opportunity, and it is notable that the threshold IQ for genius—probably around 125—is not all that high. William Shockley and Luis Walter Alvarez, who both went on to win the Nobel Prize for physics, were excluded from the

Terman Study of the Gifted on account of... their unremarkable IQ scores.

For the story, in later life Shockley developed controversial views on race and eugenics, setting off a debate over the use and applicability of IQ tests.

11
Knowledge

What if we are being radically deceived? What if I am no more than a brain kept alive in a vat and fed with stimuli by a mad scientist? What if my life is nothing but a dream or computer simulation? Like the prisoners in Plato's cave, I would be experiencing, not reality itself, but a mere facsimile or simulacrum of reality. I could not be said to know anything at all, not even that I was being deceived.

Which would you prefer: a life of limitless pleasure as a brain in a vat, or a genuine human life along with all its struggle and suffering? Most people actually opt for the latter, suggesting that we value truth and authenticity, and, by extension, that we value knowledge for its own sake, as well as for its instrumentality. If we are at all interested in reason (Chapter 9), it is because we are interested in knowledge, which is both the product and the raw material of reason.

But even if we are not being radically deceived, it is not at all clear that we can have any knowledge of the world. Much of our everyday knowledge comes from the use of our senses, especially sight. 'Seeing is believing', as the saying goes. French, unlike English, is one of the many languages that have two verbs for 'to know', namely, *savoir* and *connaître*, where *connaître* implies a direct, privileged kind of knowledge acquired through sense experience. But appearances, as we all know, can be deceptive: a stick held under water appears to bend; and hot tarmac, when viewed from a distance, looks like sparkling water. Our senses are subject to manipulation, as, for example, when a garden designer uses focal points or clever planting to create an illusion of space. An illusion is a sense percept that arises as the misrepresentation of a stimulus, such as hearing voices in rustling leaves; whereas a hallucination is a sense percept that arises in the absence of a stimulus, such as hearing voices even though there are no other sounds or people within our sensory field. According to one large population study carried out in the UK and Germany, almost 40% of people have experienced, not mere illusions, but hallucinations of some kind. My mind interprets a certain wavelength as the colour red, but another animal or even another person may interpret it as something entirely other, or perhaps not perceive it at all. A bat or a salmon experiences the world very differently to me. And what about you? How do I know that what I experience as pain is also what you experience as pain? You may react as I do, but that need not mean that you are minded like I am, or even that you are minded at all. All I might know is how the world appears to me, not how the world actually is.

Beyond my immediate environment, much of what I count as knowledge is so-called testimonial knowledge, that is, knowledge gained by the say-so of others, often teachers, writers, and journalists. How do I know that the earth revolves around the sun and not the sun around the earth? Only because I've been told, many times over. If a piece of testimonial knowledge conflicts with my worldview, I tend, in the absence of non-testimonial evidence, to check it against other forms of testimony. If a friend tells me that Melbourne is the most populous city in Australia, I might search the Internet and find that it is actually Sydney, even though I have never been to Australia and cannot be sure of what I read on the Internet.

Knowing that the earth revolves around the sun and that Sydney is the most populous city in Australia are cases of declarative (or propositional) knowledge, knowledge that can be expressed in declarative sentences or propositions. I know, or think that I know, that 'my keys are in my pocket', 'Quito is the capital of Ecuador', and 'Prince Harry is married to Meghan Markle'. Apart from declarative knowledge, I also have know-how, for example, I know how to cook and how to drive a car. The relationship between knowing that and knowing how is not entirely clear, but it may be that knowing how collapses into multiple instances of knowing that.

For me to know that something, for example, that Mount Athos is in Greece, it must be the case that (1) I believe that Mount Athos is in Greece, and (2) Mount Athos actually is in Greece. In short, knowledge is true belief. True beliefs are better than false beliefs because they are, on average, more useful. Some true beliefs are more useful than others. For example, my true belief that my wine has been poisoned is more useful than my true belief that my neighbour has 423 stamps in her collection. A few true beliefs, such as the true belief that I am a coward, can actually be unhelpful, not to mention unpleasant, and I deploy a number of psychological mechanisms, or ego defences, to keep such beliefs out of my conscious mind (Chapter 5). Conversely, some false beliefs, such as that my country or football team is somehow special, can be helpful, at least to my fragile self-esteem. But, on the whole, we should seek to maximize our true beliefs, especially our useful or otherwise valuable true beliefs, while minimizing our false beliefs.

If knowledge is true belief, it is not any kind of true belief. People with paranoid psychosis often form the belief that they are being persecuted, for example, that government agents are trying to kill them. Clearly, this cannot count as knowledge, even if it somehow happens to be true. Beliefs that are held on inadequate grounds, but by chance happen to be true, fall short of knowledge. In the *Meno*, Plato compares such 'correct opinions' to the statues of Dædalus, which run away unless they can be tied down 'with an account of the reason why', whereupon they become knowledge. Knowledge is not merely true belief, but *justified* true belief. Knowledge as justified true belief is called the tripartite, or three-part, theory of knowledge. Setting aside any intrinsic value that it may have, knowledge (justified true belief) is better than mere true belief in that it is more stable and reliable, and therefore more useful.

Fine, but what does justification demand? I justify my belief in manmade global warming by the current scientific consensus as reported by the press. But what justifies my belief in the current scientific consensus, or in the press reports that I have read? Justification seems to open up an infinite regress, such that our 'justified' true beliefs can have no solid foundation to rest upon. It may be that some of our beliefs rest upon certain self-justifying foundational beliefs such as Descartes's famous 'I think therefore I am' (although even that statement is open to doubt). But few beliefs are of this kind, and those that are seem unrelated to the bulk of my beliefs. In practice, most of our beliefs seem to rest upon a circular or circuitous chain of justification, which, if large enough, might be held to constitute adequate justification. The problem, though, is that people can choose to live in different circles.

People often justify their beliefs by means of arguments. As we have seen (Chapter 1), there are two broad kinds of argument, deductive and inductive. In a deductive or 'truth-preserving' argument, the conclusion follows from the premises as their logical consequence. In an inductive argument, the conclusion is merely supported or suggested by the premises. A third form of reasoning, abduction, involves inference to the best explanation for an observation or set of observations, for example, a doctor diagnosing a disease from a constellation of symptoms. But once broken down, abductive reasoning is no other than a shorthand form of inductive reasoning. Of course, arguments, whether deductive or inductive, may or may not be fallacious (Chapter 2). But there is an even deeper problem, which is the Problem of Induction, first visited in Chapter 9. Induction is both unsafe and unsupported, prompting CD Broad to call it 'the glory of science and the scandal of philosophy'. This is an even bigger problem than it seems, since inductive arguments usually supply the premises for deductive arguments. In the words of CA Strong:

> *A philosopher is commonly thought of as a reasoner, but I would rather conceive him as a person who is careful in his assumptions. The most agile reasoners are sometimes indifferent or not sufficiently careful as to their premises, in accordance with Mr Russell's [Bertrand Russell] mot that a mathematician is a man who does not know what he is talking about or care whether what he says is true, so long as it is correctly reasoned.*

All this to say that justification is hard to come by. But there is another problem lurking in the tripartite theory of knowledge. In 1963, Edmund Gettier published a short paper showing that it is possible to hold a justified true belief without this amounting to knowledge! Here is my own example of a Gettier-like case. Suppose I am sleeping in my bed one night. Suddenly, I hear someone trying to unlock the front door. I call the police to share my belief that I am about to be burgled. One minute later, the police arrive and apprehend a burglar at my door. But it was not the burglar who made the noise: it was a drunken student who, coming home from a party, mistook my house for his own. While my belief was both true and justified, I did not, properly speaking, have knowledge. Responses to the Gettier problem typically involve elaborating upon the tripartite theory, for example, stipulating that luck or false evidence should not be involved. But such riders seem to place the bar for knowledge far too high.

As Gettier made clear, it is not so easy to identify instances of knowledge. Instead of defining the criteria for knowledge and, from these criteria, identifying instances of knowledge, it might be easier to work the other way, that is, begin by identifying instances of knowledge and, from these instances, derive the criteria for knowledge. But how can we identify instances of knowledge without having first defined the criteria for knowledge? And how can we define the criteria for knowledge without having first identified instances of knowledge? This is the Catch 22, which, in one form or other, seems to lie at the bottom of the problem of knowledge.

Plato's allegory of the cave

Human beings spend all their lives in an underground cave with its mouth open towards the light. They have their legs and necks shackled so that they can only see in front of them, towards the back of the cave. Above and behind them, a fire is blazing. Between them and the fire is a low wall behind which men carry diverse statues above their heads, and the fire casts the shadows of these statues onto the back of the cave. Because the shadows are all they ever see, the prisoners suppose that the shadows are the objects themselves.

If a prisoner is unshackled and turned towards the light, he suffers sharp pains, but in time begins to discern the statues. He is then dragged out of the cave, where the light is so bright that he can only look at the shadows, and then at the reflections, and then finally at the objects themselves, of which the statues were but pale imitations. In time, he looks up at the sun, and understands that the sun is the cause of everything that he sees around him, of light, and sight, and the objects of sight.

Figure 5: Plato's cave. Engraving by Jan Saenredam, c. 1600.

The purpose of education is to drag the prisoner as far out of the cave as possible; not merely to instil knowledge into his soul, but to turn his whole soul towards the sun, which is the Form of the Good.

Once outside, the prisoner is reluctant to go back into the cave and involve himself in human affairs. If he will not, he must be made to go back down and partake of human labours and honours, because the State aims at the happiness not of a single person or class but of all its citizens. What's more, the freed prisoner has a duty to give service to the State, since it was by the State that he was educated to see the light of the sun.

The State in which the rulers are most reluctant to govern is always the best and most quietly governed, and the State in which they are most eager, the worst... You must contrive for your future rulers another and a better life than that of a ruler, and then you may have a well ordered State; for only in the State which offers this, will they rule who are truly rich, not in silver and gold, but in virtue and wisdom, which are the true blessings of life... And the only life which looks down upon the life of political ambition is that of true philosophy. Do you know of any other?

12

Memory

In *Game of Thrones*, Archmæster Ebrose says to Samwell:

> In the Citadel, we lead different lives for different reasons. We are this world's memory, Samwell Tarly. Without us, men would be little better than dogs. Don't remember any meal but the last, can't see forward to any but the next. And every time you leave the house and shut the door, they howl like you're gone forever.

Later, during a war council, Bran Stark reveals that the Night King is after him because he is the Three-Eyed Raven that embodies the collective memory of mankind: 'An endless night. He wants to erase this world. And I am its memory.' 'That's what death is, isn't it?' replies Samwell, 'Forgetting, being forgotten. People forget where we've been and what we've done, we're not men anymore, just animals...'

Memory refers to the system, or systems, by which the mind registers, stores, and retrieves information for the purpose of optimizing future action.

Memory can be divided into short-term and long-term, with long-term memory further divided into episodic and semantic.

Episodic memory records sense experience, while semantic memory records abstract facts and concepts. The distinction between episodic and semantic memory is implicit in a number of languages in which the verb 'to know' has two forms, for example, in French, *connaître* and *savoir*, where *connaître* implies a direct, privileged kind of knowledge.

There is, naturally, a close connection between memory and knowledge. Recall from Chapter 11 that the *connaître/savoir* dichotomy also pertains to the theory of knowledge, which distinguishes between first-hand knowledge gained through direct sense experience and testimonial knowledge gained by the say-so of others, often teachers, writers, and journalists. In the absence of first-hand knowledge, the accuracy of a piece of testimony can only be verified against other sources of testimony. Similarly, the accuracy of most memories can only be verified against other memories. For the vast majority of memories, there is no independent standard.

Episodic and semantic memory are held to be explicit or 'declarative', but there is also a third kind of memory, procedural memory, which is implicit or unconscious, for skills such as reading, slicing vegetables, and riding a bicycle. If episodic memory broadly corresponds to first-hand knowledge and semantic memory to testimonial knowledge, then procedural memory corresponds to know-how. Although held to be explicit, episodic and semantic memory can influence action without any need for conscious retrieval or processing—which is, of course, the aim of practices such as advertising and brainwashing. Try though I might, I can only bring up a handful of memories from my holiday to Uruguay last year, and even fewer from the entire year 2010. Most of our memories lie beyond or beneath conscious retrieval, locked up in a dark cellar with almost no chance of ever escaping.

Memory is mysterious, even miraculous: organic brain matter somehow re-arranges itself to encode experiences, facts, and procedures. The most mysterious and miraculous type of memory is prospective memory, or 'remembering to remember'. To ring my mother on her birthday, I must not only remember her birthday, but also remember to remember it. Whenever I forget to set my alarm clock, I find myself waking up just in time to make my appointment or catch my flight, even when I have slept only three or four hours. This suggests that, even in sleep, the mind is able to remember to remember, and able to keep track of time.

Memory is encoded across several brain areas, meaning that brain damage or disease can affect one type of memory more than others. For example, Korsakov syndrome, which results from severe thiamine deficiency (most commonly a feature of alcohol dependency) and consequent damage to the mammillary bodies and dorsomedial nucleus of the thalamus, affects episodic memory more than semantic memory, and anterograde memory (ability to form new memories) more than retrograde memory (store of old memories), while sparing short-term and procedural memory. Alzheimer's disease on the other hand affects short-term memory more than long-term memory, at least in the earlier stages of the disease.

As a psychiatrist, I am often asked to assess people with dementia, making me all too aware of the importance of memory in daily life. To live without memory is to live in a perpetual present, without past and without future, going through the same thoughts, the same questions, the same fears, over and over and over again. Without any memory at all, it would be impossible to: speak, read, learn, find one's way, make decisions, identify or use objects, cook, wash, dress, or develop and maintain relationships. More fundamentally, it would be impossible to know anything, and therefore to reason, which is the process of building knowledge from knowledge. Without memory, it would be impossible to build upon anything or engage in any form of sustained goal-directed activity. In Greek myth, the goddess of memory, Mnemosyne, lay with Zeus for nine consecutive nights, thereby begetting the nines Muses. Without memory, there would be no art or science, no craft or culture… and no meaning either.

Nostalgia, sentimentality for the past, is often prompted by feelings of loneliness, disconnectedness, or meaninglessness. Revisiting the past can lend us much needed context, perspective, and direction, reminding and reassuring us that our life is not as banal as it might seem, that it is rooted in a narrative, and that there have been—and will once again be—meaningful moments and memories. Judging by the cost and logistics of a wedding and wedding photographs, we are prepared to go to great lengths to manufacture meaningful moments and memories. But people with severe memory loss can no longer revisit the past and may instead resort to confabulation (the making up of memories) to create the meaning and identity that they crave. I once visited a nursing home in southern England to assess an 85-year-old lady with advanced Alzheimer's disease. She insisted that we were in a hotel in Marbella: she was planning her wedding and wouldn't have time to talk to me. When I asked her, 'What did you do yesterday?' she replied, with a twinkle in her eye, 'I hit the town for my hen night and my friends spoilt me rotten with champagne and fancy cocktails.'

Bernard Ingram, Margaret Thatcher's former press secretary, recently revealed that, after the Iron Lady developed dementia, 'it was as though nothing had changed from Number 10':

> When I went to see her she'd say, 'Will you have a coffee and sit down'. Then she looks at me expectantly, 'What is the problem?' So on the way in on the train, I always acquired a problem from reading the papers. And we discussed this problem at least six times in the hour, because she'd forgotten. It would have been funny if it weren't tragic. Then she'd say, 'Why have we got into this mess? But, more importantly, and what are we going to do about it?'

The search for meaning is deeply ingrained in human nature, so much so that, when pressed to define man, Plato replied simply, 'a being in search of meaning.' Memory is meaning, forgetting is death, and the job of the writer is not so much to teach as to remind.

But, of course, memory is not all that reliable. It could be argued that, like confabulation, nostalgia is a form of self-deception, in that it involves distortion and idealization of the past. The Romans had a tag for the phenomenon that psychologists have come to call 'rosy retrospection': *memoria praeteritorum bonorum*, 'the past is always well remembered.' And memory is unreliable in other ways as well. 'Everyone' said John Barth, 'is necessarily the hero of his own life story.' We curate our memories by consolidating those that confirm or conform with our idea of self, while discarding or distorting those that conflict with it. We are very likely to remember events of existential significance such as our first kiss or first day at school—and, of course, it helps that we often rehearse those memories. Even then, we remember only one or two scenes, and only the main elements, and fill in the gaps and background with reconstructed or 'averaged' memories. *Déjà-vu*, the feeling that an ongoing situation has already been experienced, may arise from a near match between the ongoing situation and an averaged memory of that sort of situation. Our memories are filtered through and distorted by our interests and emotions. Two people supporting opposing football teams or political parties will register and recall very different things and likely disagree about 'the facts'. In the UK in the aftermath of the 2019 European Elections, both 'leavers' and 'remainers' claimed to have won the ballot.

Broadly speaking, emotionally charged events are more likely to be remembered, and it has been found that injections of cortisol or epinephrine (adrenaline) can improve retention rates. But if a situation is highly stressful, memory may be impaired as cognitive resources are diverted to dealing with the situation, for example, escaping from the gunman rather than registering his clothing or facial features. In addition, any attention paid to the gunman is likely to focus on the gun itself, leading to a species of peripheral blindness. This, of course, has important implications for the accuracy of eyewitness testimony, which might also be distorted by the use of leading or loaded questions. In a famous study, *Reconstruction of Automobile Destruction* [sic.], Loftus and Palmer asked people to estimate the speed of motor vehicles at their point of impact and found that the verb used in the question ('smashed', 'collided', 'bumped', 'hit', or 'contacted') altered perceptions of speed. In addition, those who had been asked the 'smashed' question were more likely to report having seen broken glass. After a traumatic event, in response to unbearable stress, a person might go so far as to dissociate from the event, for example, by losing all memory for the event (dissociative amnesia) or even, as Agatha Christie famously did, assuming another identity and departing on a sudden, unexpected journey (dissociative fugue). So heightened emotion improves memory, but severe stress and trauma impede it.

Of all the senses, it is the sense of smell that triggers the most vivid memories, even when these are from the very distant past. The olfactory bulb has direct connections to the amygdala and hippocampus, which are heavily involved in memory and emotion. These three structures—the olfactory bulb, the amygdala, and the hippocampus—form part of the limbic system, a ring of phylogenetically primitive, 'paleomammalian' cortex that is the seat of memory, emotion, and motivation. In a famous passage now referred to as 'the madeleine moment', Marcel Proust describes the uncanny ability of certain smells to recapture the 'essence of the past':

> No sooner had the warm liquid mixed with the crumbs touched my palate that a shudder ran through me and I stopped, intent upon the extraordinary thing that was happening to me. An exquisite pleasure had invaded my senses, something isolated, detached, with no suggestion of its origin. And at once the vicissitudes of life had become indifferent to me, its disasters innocuous, its brevity illusory—this new sensation having had on me the effect which love has of filling me with a precious essence; or rather this essence was not in me it was me. ... Whence did it come? What did it mean? How could I seize and apprehend it? ... And suddenly the memory revealed itself. The taste was that of the little piece of madeleine which on Sunday mornings at Combray (because on those mornings I did not go out before mass), when I went to say good morning to her in her bedroom, my aunt Léonie used to give me, dipping it first in her own cup of tea or tisane. The sight of the little madeleine had recalled nothing to my mind before I tasted it. And all from my cup of tea.

Killing two birds with one stone, here are ten ways to improve your memory that also shed light on its workings.

1. *Get plenty of sleep.* If you read a book or article when very tired, you will forget most of what you have read. Sleep improves attention and concentration, and therefore the registration of information. And sleep is also required for memory consolidation.

2. *Pay attention.* You cannot take in information unless you are paying attention, and you cannot memorize information unless you are taking it in. It helps if you are actually interested in the material, so try to develop an interest in everything! As Einstein said, 'There are only two ways to live your life. One is as though nothing is a miracle. The other is as though everything is a miracle.'

3. *Involve as many senses as you can.* For instance, if you are sitting in a lecture, jot down a few notes. If you are reading a chapter or article, read it aloud to yourself and inject some drama into your performance.

4. *Structure information.* If you need to remember a list of ingredients, think of them under the subheadings of starter, main, and dessert, and visualize the number of ingredients under each subheading. If you need to remember a telephone number, think of it in terms of the first five digits, the middle three digits, and the last three digits—or whatever works best.

5. *Process information.* If possible, summarize the material in your own words. Or reorganize it so that it is easier to learn. With more complex material, try to understand its meaning and significance. Shakespearean actors find it much easier to remember their lines if they can understand and feel them. If needs must, concentrate on the important things, or the bigger picture. In the words of Oscar Wilde, 'One should absorb the colour of life, but one should never remember its details. Details are always vulgar.'

6. *Relate information to what you already know.* New information is much easier to remember if it can be contextualized. A recent study looking at the role of high-level processes found that chess knowledge predicts chess memory (memory of the layout of a particular chess game) even after controlling for chess experience.

7. *Use mnemonics.* Tie information to visual images, sentences, and acronyms. For example, you might remember that your hairdresser is called Sharon by picturing a rose of Sharon or Sharon fruit. Or you might remember the colours of the rainbow and their order by the sentence, 'Richard Of York Gave Battle In Vain.'

8. *Rehearse.* Sleep on the information and review it the following day. Then review it at increasing intervals until you feel comfortable with it. Memories fade if not rehearsed, or are overlain by other memories and can no longer be accessed.

9. *Be aware of context.* It is easier to retrieve a memory if you find yourself in a similar situation, or similar state of mind, to the one in which the memory was laid. People with low mood tend to recall their losses and failures while overlooking their strengths and achievements. If one day you pass the cheesemonger in the street, you may not, without her usual apron and array of cheeses, immediately recognize her, even though you are otherwise familiar with her. You might even say something like, 'Gosh, remind me, where do I know you from?' If you are preparing for an exam, try to recreate the conditions of the exam: for example, sit at a similar desk, at a similar time of day, and use ink on paper.

10. *Be creative.* Bizarre or unusual experiences, facts, and associations are easier to remember. Because unfamiliar experiences stick in the mind, trips and holidays give the impression of 'living', and, by extension, of having lived for longer.

Our life is just as long or short as our remembering: as rich as our imagining, as vibrant as our feeling, and as profound as our thinking.

13

Science

If knowledge is so iffy, what of science? It is sometimes said that 90 percent of scientists who ever lived are alive today, so why is science not advancing by leaps and bounds?

To call a thing 'scientific' or 'scientifically proven' is to lend that thing instant credibility. Especially in Northern Europe, more people believe in science than in religion, and attacking science can raise the same old atavistic defences. In a bid to emulate, or at least evoke, the apparent success of physics, many areas of study have claimed the mantle of science: economic science, political science, social science, and so on. Whether or not these disciplines are true, *bona fide* sciences is a matter for debate, since there are in fact no clear or reliable criteria for distinguishing a science from a non-science.

What might be said is that all sciences (unlike, say, magic or myth) share certain assumptions which underpin the *scientific method*—in particular, that there is an objective reality governed by uniform laws, and that this reality can be discovered by systematic observation. A scientific experiment is basically a repeatable procedure designed to help support or refute a particular hypothesis about the nature of reality.

Typically, it seeks to isolate the element under investigation by eliminating or 'controlling for' other variables that may be confused or 'confounded' with the element under investigation. Important assumptions or expectations include: all potential confounding factors can be identified and controlled for; any measurements are appropriate and sensitive to the element under investigation; and the results are analysed and interpreted rationally and impartially.

Still, many things can go wrong with the experiment. For example, with drug trials, experiments that have not been adequately randomized (when subjects are randomly allocated to test and control groups) or adequately blinded (when information about the drug administered/received is withheld from the investigator/subject) significantly exaggerate the benefits of treatment. Investigators may consciously or subconsciously withhold or ignore data that does not meet their desires or expectations ('cherry picking') or stray beyond their original hypothesis to look for chance or uncontrolled correlations ('data dredging'). A promising result, which might have been obtained by chance, is much more likely to be published than an unfavourable one ('publication bias'), creating the false impression that most studies on the drug have been positive, and therefore that the drug is much more effective than it actually is. One damning systematic review found that, compared to independently funded drug trials, those funded by pharmaceutical companies are less likely to be published; while those that are published are *four times* more likely to feature positive results for the products of their sponsors!

So much for the easy, superficial problems. But there are deeper, more intractable philosophical problems as well. For most of recorded history, 'knowledge' was based on authority, especially that of the Bible and white-beards such as Aristotle, Ptolemy, and Galen. But today, or so we like to think, knowledge is much more secure because grounded in observation. Putting to one side that much of what counts as scientific knowledge cannot be directly observed, and that our species-specific senses are partial and limited, there is, in that phrase of NR Hanson, 'more to seeing than meets the eyeball':

> *Seeing is an experience. A retinal reaction is only a physical state ... People, not their eyes, see. Cameras and eyeballs are blind.*

Observation involves both perception and cognition, with sensory information filtered, interpreted, and even distorted by factors such as beliefs, experience, expectations, desires, and emotions. The finished product of observation is then encoded into a statement of fact consisting of linguistic symbols and concepts, each one with its own particular history, connotations, and limitations. All this means that it is impossible to test a hypothesis in isolation from all the background theories, frameworks, and assumptions from which it arises.

This is important, because, as you will remember from Chapters 9 and 11, science principally proceeds by induction— that is, by the observation of large and representative samples. But even if observation could be objective, observations alone, no matter how accurate and exhaustive, cannot in themselves establish the validity of a hypothesis. How do we know that flamingos are pink? Well, we don't know for sure. We merely suppose that they are because, so far, every flamingo that we have seen has been pink. But the existence of a non-pink flamingo is not beyond the bounds of possibility. A turkey that is fed every morning might infer by induction that it will carry on being fed every morning, until on Christmas Eve the goodly farmer corners it and wrings its neck. As I said in Chapter 9, inductive reasoning only ever yields probabilistic 'truths', and yet it is the basis of everything that we know or think that we know about the world we live in. Our only justification for induction is that it has worked in the past, which is, of course, an inductive proof, tantamount to saying that induction works because induction works.

It may be that science proceeds not by induction, but by abduction, or finding the most likely explanation for the observations—as, for example, when a physician is faced with a constellation of symptoms and formulates a 'working diagnosis' that more or less fits the clinical picture (Chapter 11). But ultimately abduction is no more than a type of 'backward reasoning', formally equivalent to the logical fallacy of affirming the consequent (Chapter 1).

> *If A, then B.*
> *B.*
> *Therefore, A.*

> *If I have indigestion, then I have central chest pain.*
> *I have central chest pain.*
> *Therefore, I have indigestion.*

But, of course, I could also be having angina, a myocardial infarction, a pulmonary embolism... How am I to decide between these possibilities? At medical school we were taught that 'common things are common'. This is a formulation of Ockham's razor, which involves choosing the simplest available explanation. Ockham's razor, also called the law of parsimony, is often invoked as a principle of inductive reasoning, but of course the simplest explanation is not necessarily the best or correct one, and the universe is proving much more mysterious than we might have imagined, or even been able to imagine, just a generation ago. What's more, we may be unable to decide which is the simplest explanation, or even what 'simple' might mean in context. Some people think that God is the simplest explanation for creation, while others think that the concept of God is rather far-fetched. Still, there is some wisdom in Ockham's razor: while the simplest explanation may not be the correct one, neither should we labour or keep on 'fixing' a preferred hypothesis to save it from a simpler, neater explanation. [I should mention in passing that the psychological equivalent of Ockham's razor is Hanlon's razor: never attribute to malice that which can be adequately explained by neglect, incompetence, or stupidity.]

Simpler hypotheses are also preferable in that they are easier to disprove. To rescue it from the problems raised by induction, Karl Popper argued that science proceeds not inductively but deductively, by making bold claims and then seeking to disprove, or falsify, those claims.

> *'All flamingos are pink.' Oh, but look, here's a flamingo that's not pink. Therefore, it is not the case that all flamingos are pink.*

On this account, theories such as those of Freud and Marx are not scientific in so far as they cannot be falsified. But if Popper is right in holding that science proceeds by deductive falsification, then science could never tell us what is, but only ever what is not. Even if we did land on some truth, we could never know for sure that we had arrived. Another issue with falsification is that when the hypothesis conflicts with the data, it could be the data rather than the hypothesis that is at fault— in which case it would be a mistake to reject the hypothesis. Scientists need to be dogmatic enough to persevere with a preferred hypothesis in the face of apparent falsifications, but not so dogmatic as to cling to their preferred hypothesis in the face of robust and repeated falsifications. It's a delicate balance to strike.

For Thomas Kuhn, scientific hypotheses are shaped and restricted by the worldview, or paradigm, within which scientists operate. Most scientists are as blind to the paradigm as fish to water, and unable to see across or beyond it. In fact, most of the clinical medical students I teach at Oxford, and who already have a science degree, don't even know what the word 'paradigm' means. When data emerges that conflicts with the paradigm, it is usually discarded, dismissed, or disregarded. But nothing lasts forever: after much resistance and burning at the stake (whether literal or metaphorical), the paradigm gradually weakens and is overturned. Examples of such 'paradigm shifts' include the transition from Aristotelian mechanics to classical mechanics, the transition from miasma theory to the germ theory of disease, and the transition from clinical judgement to evidence-based medicine. In 1949, Egas Moniz received a Nobel Prize for his discovery of 'the therapeutic value of leucotomy in certain psychoses'. Today, prefrontal leucotomy (also called lobotomy), which involves the surgical severance of most of the connections to and from the prefrontal cortex of the brain, is derided as a barbaric treatment from a much darker age. Of course, a paradigm does not die overnight. Reason is, for the most part, a tool that we use to justify what we are already inclined or programmed to believe, and a human life cannot easily accommodate more than one paradigm. In the words of Max Planck,

> *A new scientific truth does not triumph by convincing its opponents and making them see the light, but rather because its opponents eventually die, and a new generation grows up that is familiar with it.*

Or to put it more pithily, science advances one funeral at a time.

In the *Structure of Scientific Revolutions*, Kuhn argued that rival paradigms offer competing and irreconcilable accounts of reality, implying that there are no independent standards by which they might be judged against one another. Imre Lakatos sought to reconcile and in some sense rescue Popper and Kuhn, and spoke of programs rather than paradigms. A program is based on a hard core of theoretical assumptions accompanied by more modest auxiliary hypotheses formulated to protect the hard core against any conflicting data. While the hard core cannot be abandoned without jeopardizing the program, auxiliary hypotheses can be adapted to protect the hard core against evolving threats, rendering the hard core unfalsifiable. A progressive program is one in which changes to auxiliary hypotheses lead to greater predictive power, strengthening the whole, whereas a degenerative program is one in which these *ad hoc* elaborations become sterile and cumbersome. A degenerative program, says Lakatos, is one which is ripe for replacement. For example, classical mechanics, with Newton's three laws of motions at the core, though very popular in in its time, came under increasing peripheral strain and was gradually superseded by the special theory of relativity.

For Paul Feyerabend, Lakatos's theory makes a mockery of any pretence at scientific rationality or objectivity. Feyerabend went so far as to call Lakatos a 'fellow anarchist', albeit one in disguise. For Feyerabend, there is no such thing as 'a' or 'the' scientific method: *anything goes*, and, as a form of knowledge, science is no more privileged than magic, myth, or religion. More than that, science has come to occupy the same place in the human psyche as religion once did. Although science began as a liberating movement, it grew dogmatic and repressive, more of an ideology than a rational method that leads to ineluctable progress. To quote Feyerabend:

Knowledge is not a series of self-consistent theories that converges towards an ideal view; it is rather an ever increasing ocean of mutually incompatible (and perhaps even incommensurable) alternatives, each single theory, each fairy tale, each myth that is part of the collection forcing the others into greater articulation and all of them contributing, via this process of competition, to the development of our consciousness.

Feyerabend was never one for mashing or mincing his words. 'My life' he wrote 'has been the result of accidents, not of goals and principles. My intellectual work forms only an insignificant part of it. Love and personal understanding are much more important. Leading intellectuals with their zeal for objectivity kill these personal elements. They are criminals, not the leaders of mankind.'

Every paradigm that has come and gone is now deemed to have been false, inaccurate, or incomplete, and it would be ignorant or arrogant or both to assume that our current ones might amount to the truth, the whole truth, and nothing but the truth. If our aim in doing science is merely to make predictions and promote successful outcomes, then this may not matter quite so much, and we continue to use outdated or discredited theories such as Newton's laws of motion so long as we find them useful. But it would help if we could be more realistic about science and, at the same time, more rigorous, imaginative, and open-minded in conducting it.

14

Truth

In Plato's *Cratylus*, on the philosophy of language, Socrates says that *aletheia* [Greek, 'truth'] is a compression of the phrase 'a wandering that is divine'. Since Plato, many thinkers have spoken of truth and God in the same breath, and truth has also been linked with concepts such as justice, power, and freedom. According to John the Apostle, Jesus said to the Jews: 'And ye shall know the truth, and the truth shall make you free.'

Today, God may be dying, but what about truth? Rudy Giuliani, Donald Trump's personal lawyer, claimed that 'truth isn't truth', while Kellyanne Conway, Trump's counsellor, presented the public with what she called 'alternative facts'. Over in the UK in the run-up to the Brexit referendum, Michael Gove, then Minister of Justice and Lord Chancellor, opined that people 'have had enough of experts' (Chapter 2, genetic fallacy).

Following his defeat at the Battle of Actium in 31 BC, Mark Antony heard a rumour that Cleopatra had committed suicide and, in consequence, stabbed himself in the abdomen—only to discover that Cleopatra herself had been responsible for spreading the rumour. He later died in her arms. 'Fake news' is nothing new, but in our Internet age it has spread like a disease, swinging elections, fomenting social unrest, undermining institutions, and diverting political capital away from health, education, and good government. Initially, 'fake news' referred to false news with large scale popular traction, although Trump seems to have broadened the definition to include any news that is unfavourable to him.

Those who are alarmed, or who despair, might take some comfort in the words of Søren Kierkegaard:

> *Truth always rests with the minority, and the minority is always stronger than the majority, because the minority is generally formed by those who really have an opinion, while the strength of a majority is illusory, formed by the gangs who have no opinion—and who, therefore, in the next instant (when it is evident that the minority is the stronger) assume its opinion... while truth again reverts to a new minority.*

As we have discovered, neither logic nor reason nor science, though they take it for a given, can guarantee the truth. But what is truth, and how, if at all, can we attain to it?

One way to understand truth is simply to look at its opposite, or opposites, namely, lies and bullshit. Lies differ from bullshit in that the liar must track the truth in order to conceal it, whereas the bullshitter has no regard or sensitivity for the truth or even for what his or her audience believes. In the words of Harry Frankfurt:

> *Someone who lies and someone who tells the truth are playing on opposite sides, so to speak, in the same game. Each responds to the facts as he understands them, although the response of the one is guided by the authority of the truth, while the response of the other defies that authority and refuses to meet its demands. The bullshitter ignores these demands altogether. He does not reject the authority of the truth, as the liar does, and oppose himself to it. He pays no attention to it at all. By virtue of this, bullshit is a greater enemy of the truth than lies are.*

Truth is a property not so much of thoughts and ideas but more properly of beliefs and assertions. But to believe or assert something is not enough to make it true, or else the claim that 'to believe something makes it true' would be just as true as the claim that 'to believe something does not make it true'. For centuries, philosophers have agreed that thought or language is true if it corresponds to an independent reality. For Aristotle, 'to say that what is is, and what is not is not, is true.' For Avicenna, truth is 'what corresponds in the mind to what is outside it'. And for Aquinas, it is 'the adequation of things and the intellect' [*adæquatio rei et intellectus*]. Unfortunately for this so-called correspondence theory of truth, the mind does not perceive reality as it is, but only as it can, filtering, distorting, and interpreting it. In modern times, it has been argued that truth is constructed by social and cultural processes, to say nothing of individual desires and dispositions. Michel Foucault famously spoke, not of truth or truths, but of 'regimes of truth'. Categories and constructs concerning, for example, race, sexuality, and mental disorder may not reflect biological let alone metaphysical realities.

According to the coherence theory of truth, a thing is more likely to be true if it fits comfortably into a large and coherent system of beliefs. It remains that the system could be a giant fiction, entirely detached from reality, but this becomes increasingly unlikely as we investigate, curate, and add to its components—assuming, and it is quite an assumption, that we are operating in good faith, with truth, rather than self-preservation or -aggrandizement, as our aim. Thus conceived, truth is not a property, or merely a property, but an attitude, a way of being in the world. Martin Heidegger appears to take this idea further still:

> 'Truth' is not a feature of correct propositions which are asserted of an 'object' by a human 'subject' and then are 'valid' somewhere, in what sphere we know not. Rather, truth is disclosure of beings through which an openness essentially unfolds. All human comportment and bearing are exposed in its open region.

All the better if we can actually do something useful with our system and its components. According to the pragmatic theory of truth, truth leads to successful action; therefore, successful action is an indicator of truth. Clearly, we could not have sent a rocket to the moon if our science had been wide off the mark. For William James, the truth is 'only the expedient in the way of our thinking, just as the right is only the expedient in the way of our behaving'. If something works, it may well be true; if it doesn't, it most probably isn't. But what if something works for me but not for you? Is that thing then true for me but not for you? For Nietzsche, who made himself the natural ally of two-penny tyrants, truth is power, and power truth: 'The falseness of a judgement is not necessarily an objection to a judgement... The question is to what extent it is life-advancing, life-preserving, species-preserving, perhaps even species-breeding...' Short-term or long-term, Freddy, and at what cost?

That a thing fits into a system, or leads to successful action, may suggest that it is true, but does not tell us much about what truth actually is, while the correspondence theory of truth is so thin as to be almost or entirely tautological. And perhaps for a reason. It has been argued that to say that 'X is true' is merely to say that X, and therefore that truth is an empty predicate. Truth is not a real property of things. Rather, it is a feature of language used to emphasize, agree, or hypothesize, or for stylistic purposes. For example, it can be used to explicate the Catholic dogma of papal infallibility: 'Everything that the pope says is true'. But this is merely shorthand for saying that if the Pope says A, then it is the case that A; and if he says B, then B...

For some thinkers, something can only be true or false if it is open to verification, at least in theory if not also in practice. The truth of something lies at the end of our inquiry into that thing. But as our inquiry can have no end, the truth of something can never be more than our best opinion of that thing. If best opinion is all that we can have or hope for, then best opinion is as good as truth, and truth is a redundant concept. But best opinion is only best because, at least on average, it is closest to the truth, which, as well as instrumental value, has deep intrinsic value.

Some practical advice

A reader once emailed me to ask, 'how can I know when I am lying to myself'?

And this was my reply.

By its very nature self-deception is hard to distinguish from the truth—whether our internal, emotional truth or the external truth. One has to develop and trust one's intuition [Chapter 15]: what does it feel like to react in the way that I'm reacting? Does it feel calm, considered, and nuanced, or shallow and knee-jerk? Am I taking the welfare of others into consideration, or is it just all about me? Am I satisfied with, even proud of, my self-conquering effort, or am I left feeling small, anxious, or ashamed?

Self-deception doesn't 'add up' in the grand scheme of things and can easily be brought down by even superficial questioning. As with a jigsaw, try to look at the bigger picture of your life and see how the thought or reaction might fit in. Did you react from a position of strength or vulnerability? What would the person you most respect think? What would Socrates or the Dalai Lama think? Talk to other people and gather their opinions. If they disagree with you, does that make you feel angry, upset, or defensive? The coherence of your reaction speaks volumes about the character of your motives.

Finally, truth is constructive and adaptive, while lies are destructive and self-defeating. So how useful is a self-deceptive thought or reaction going to be for you? Are you just covering up an irrational fear, or helping to create a solid foundation for the future? Are you empowering yourself to fulfil your highest potential, or depriving yourself of opportunities for growth and creating further problems down the line? Is the cycle simply going to repeat itself, or will the truth, at last, make you free?

15

Intuition

So far, I have surveyed the various limitations of the rational methods that are emphasized in formal education. In the next few chapters, I'm going to look at alternative forms of cognition that can be used to support or supplant these rational methods, but that our culture tends to discount or disregard.

At a wine bar in Corsica, I ordered a glass and shared some low-key wine talk with the chap who brought it to me. After some time, I ordered another glass, and we spoke again. I like testing my intuitions, so I said, at point blank, 'You've written poetry, haven't you?' The chap, taken aback, confirmed that he did write poetry, and even that some of it had been published.

'Intuition' derives from the Latin *tuere*, 'to look at, watch over', and is related to 'tutor' and 'tuition' and perhaps also to the Sanskrit *tavas*, 'strong, powerful'. Broadly speaking, an intuition is a disposition to believe evolved without hard evidence or conscious deliberation. I say 'disposition to believe' rather than 'belief' because an intuition is usually held with less certainty or firmness than a belief; and 'believe' rather than 'know' because an intuition is not justified in the normal sense, and not necessarily true or accurate. It is not just that intuition is evolved without hard evidence or conscious deliberation, but that hard evidence and conscious deliberation can actually impede it. 'I am not absentminded' said GK Chesterton, 'it is presence of mind that makes me unaware of everything else.'

Intuition is often confused with instinct. Instinct is not a feeling about something, but a tendency towards a particular behaviour that is innate and common to the species. 'Anna stepped back, intuiting that the dog would follow its instinct and bite.' Although instincts tend to be associated with animals, human beings also have quite a few, even if they are, or can be, strongly modified by culture, temperament, and experience. Examples of human instincts include any number of phobias, territoriality, tribal loyalty, and the urge to procreate and rear their young—even in the face of all the inconveniences, compromises, and costs involved. These instincts are often disguised or sublimed, for example, tribal loyalty may find an outlet in sport, and the urge to procreate may take the more rarefied form of romantic love. Aristotle says in the *Rhetoric* that human beings have an instinct for truth, and in the *Poetics* that we have an instinct for rhythm and harmony. No doubt he overestimated us.

If intuition is not instinct, how does it operate? An intuition involves a coming together of facts, concepts, experiences, thoughts, and feelings that are loosely linked but too profuse, disparate, and peripheral for deliberate or rational processing. As this process is sub- or semi-conscious and the workings are hidden, an intuition appears to arise out of nothing, *ex nihilo*, and cannot, or at least not immediately or readily, be justified.

But what makes an intuition especially hard to support is that it is founded less on evidence and arguments as on the interconnection of things. It hangs, delicately and invisibly, like a spider's web. The surfacing of an intuition, which can also occur in dream or meditation, is usually associated with a concordant feeling such as joy or dread, or simple pride and pleasure at the supreme cognitive and human achievement that an intuition represents.

If this is how intuition works, then we can encourage intuition by expanding the number and range of our experiences, and by tearing down the psychological barriers, such as biases, fears, and taboos, that are preventing them from coalescing. We should also give ourselves more time and space for free association: my own intuitive faculty is sharpest when showering, travelling, or daydreaming, and when I am well rested. Finally, it would help if we actually believed in our ability to form intuitions. We have micro-intuitions all the time, about what to eat for breakfast, what to wear, what road to take, whom to talk to, what to say, how to respond, and so on. I call them micro-intuitions because they depend on a large number of subtle variables, and escape, or largely escape, conscious processing. But what about the macro-intuitions? Never in the history of humanity has the intuitive faculty been more neglected or devalued than in our rational-scientific age.

As a writer, some of what I think are my best lines are intuitions, and work by prompting the same open-ended associations in the reader. Similarly, in Zen practice, a kōan is a paradox or riddle that encourages the apprentice to connect the dots by subverting the rational and egotistic mind.

> One day, a monk said to Joshu, 'Master, I have just entered the monastery. Please give me instructions.'
> Joshu replied, 'Have you had your breakfast?'
> 'Yes I have.'
> 'Then wash your bowls.'
> The monk understood something.

Before reading on, try to work out what it is that the monk understood. You may have to shift gears, or pass into neutral.

...

What the monk understood is that life is to be found in all of life; that life, at all times, is right in front of us, waiting to be lived. Suddenly it is so obvious, but it is not something that the rational, task-driven mind seems able to grasp or hold on to for more than a moment.

Socrates is often upheld as a paradigm of reason and philosophy. Yet, he seldom claimed any real knowledge. All he had, he said, was a *daimonion* or 'divine something', an inner voice or sense that prevented him from making grave mistakes such as getting involved in politics or escaping Athens after his trial and conviction: 'This is the voice which I seem to hear murmuring in my ears, like the sound of the flute in the ears of the mystic.'

In Plato's *Phaedrus*, Socrates goes so far as to say:

> *Madness, provided it comes as the gift of heaven, is the channel by which we receive the greatest blessings... the men of old who gave things their names saw no disgrace or reproach in madness; otherwise they would not have connected it with the name of the noblest of arts, the art of discerning the future, and called it the manic art... So according to the evidence provided by our ancestors, madness is a nobler thing than sober sense... madness comes from God, whereas sober sense is merely human.*

In the *Meno*, which features Meno in conservation with Socrates, Plato explores the nature of virtue. After Socrates has applied his dialectic method, Meno reaches the realization that he is unable to define virtue, even though he has delivered innumerable speeches on the subject. He compares Socrates to the flat torpedo fish, which torpifies or numbs all those who come near it: 'And I think that you are very wise in not leaving Athens, for if you did in other places as you do here, you would be cast into prison as a magician.' Socrates, the paradigm of reason and philosophy, is also the very embodiment of a kōan!

Meno asks Socrates how he will look for virtue if he does not know what it is:

> *And how will you enquire, Socrates, into that which you do not know? What will you put forth as the subject of enquiry? And if you find what you want, how will you ever know that this is the thing which you did not know?*

In reply, Socrates says that he has heard from certain wise men and women 'who spoke of things divine' that the soul is immortal, has been born often, and has seen all things on earth and below. Since the soul already knows everything, 'learning' consists merely in recollecting that which is already known. Socrates traces a square in the dirt and asks one of Meno's slave boys a series of questions that prompt the uneducated boy, in effect, to derive Pythagoras' theorem. For Socrates, the boy's performance demonstrates that there is at least something to his theory.

Reason is not the only road to knowledge. In the *Nicomachean Ethics*, Aristotle says that the types of disposition [*hexis*] by which the soul can arrive at truth are five in number: [1] scientific knowledge [*episteme*], which arrives at necessary and eternal truths by deduction and induction; [2] art or technical skills [*techne*], which is a rational capacity to make; [3] practical wisdom [*phronesis*], which is a rational capacity to secure the good life, and includes the political art; [4] intuition [*nous*], which apprehends the first principles or unarticulated truths from which scientific knowledge is derived; and [5] philosophic wisdom [*sophia*], which is scientific knowledge combined with intuition of the things that are highest by nature.

What is interesting in Aristotle's schema is that scientific knowledge (and reason more broadly) is not independent of intuition. Rather, it is intuition that makes scientific knowledge possible. Centuries later, Locke made a similar point in contrasting intuition and demonstration: demonstration requires conscious steps, but each step is or should be intuitive.

At the very least, intuition underpins the reasoning process, since fundamental axioms and elementary rules of inference cannot be established by any other means—and, of course, the same is also true of our fundamental moral beliefs, of 'practical wisdom'. Today there is a summit in Antarctica that has been named 'Intuition Peak' in honour of the role of intuition in the advancement of human knowledge.

But one important caveat to climb down from this high point. If you put a right-wing person in a room with a left-wing one, or a religious person with a non-religious one, you will soon find that their intuitions conflict.

Intuition can and should be used to generate hypotheses, but never to justify claims.

16

Wisdom

Every time I utter the word 'wisdom', someone giggles or sneers. Wisdom, more so even than expertise, does not sit comfortably in a democratic, anti-elitist society. In an age dominated by science and technology, by specialization and compartmentalization, it is too loose, too grand, and too mysterious a concept. With our heads in our smartphones and tablets, in our bills and bank statements, we simply do not have the time or mental space for it.

But things were not always thus. The word 'wisdom' features 222 times in the Old Testament, which includes all of seven so-called 'wisdom books': Job, Psalms, Proverbs, Ecclesiastes, the Song of Solomon, the Book of Wisdom, and Sirach. 'For wisdom is a defence, and money is a defence: but the excellency of knowledge is, that wisdom giveth life to them that have it' (Ecclesiastes 7:12). Many things can prolong your life, but only wisdom can save it.

The word 'philosophy' literally means 'the love of wisdom', and wisdom is the overarching aim of philosophy, or, at least, ancient philosophy. In Plato's *Lysis*, Socrates tells the young Lysis that, without wisdom, he would be of no value to anyone:

'if you are wise, all men will be your friends and kindred, for you will be useful and good; but if you are not wise, neither father, nor mother, nor kindred, nor anyone else, will be your friends.' The patron goddess of Athens, the city in which the *Lysis* is set, is no less than Athena, goddess of wisdom, who sprung out from the skull of Zeus clad in full armour. Her symbol, and the symbol of wisdom, is the owl, a bird of prey which can cleave through darkness.

Indeed, 'wisdom' derives from the Proto-Indo-European root *weid-*, 'to see', and is related to a great number of words including: advice, druid, evident, guide, Hades, history, idea, idol, idyll, view, Veda, vision, and visit. In Norse mythology, the god Odin gouged out one of his eyes and offered it to Mimir in exchange for a drink from the well of knowledge and wisdom, symbolically trading one mode of perception for another, higher one.

And the very name of our species, *Homo sapiens*, signifies 'wise man'.

But what exactly is wisdom? People often speak of 'knowledge and wisdom' as though they might be closely related or even the same thing. So one hypothesis is that wisdom is knowledge, or a great deal of knowledge. If wisdom is knowledge, then it has to be a certain kind of knowledge, or else learning the phonebook, or the names of all the rivers in the world, might count as wisdom. And if wisdom is a certain kind of knowledge, then it is not scientific or technical knowledge, or else contemporary people would be wiser than even the wisest of ancient philosophers. Any twenty-first century school-leaver would be wiser than a Seneca or a Socrates.

Once upon a time, Chaerephon asked the oracle at Delphi whether there was anyone wiser than his friend Socrates, and the Pythian priestess replied that there was no one wiser. To discover the meaning of this divine utterance, Socrates questioned a number of men who laid claim to wisdom—politicians, generals, poets, craftsmen—and in each case concluded, 'I am likely to be wiser than he to this small extent, that I do not think I know what I do not know.' From then on, Socrates dedicated himself to the service of the gods by seeking out anyone who might be wise and, 'if he is not, showing him that he is not.' Over the years, he made so many enemies by his questioning that the Athenians condemned him to death—which served his purposes well, since it made him immortal. Today, Socrates is chiefly remembered by his death, with Seneca going so far as to opine that 'it was the hemlock that made Socrates great' [*cicuta magnum Socratem fecit*].

The Bible tells us, 'When pride comes, then comes disgrace, but with humility comes wisdom'. Socrates was the wisest of all people not because he knew everything or anything, but because he knew what he did not know—or, more subtly, because he knew the limits of the little that he did know. In fact, the world really came together in the fifth century BC, with both Confucius and the Buddha echoing from afar the words of Socrates.

> *The only true wisdom is in knowing you know nothing.*
> —*Socrates*

> *Real knowledge is to know the extent of one's own ignorance.*
> —Confucius

> *A fool who recognizes his own ignorance is thereby in fact a wise man.*
> —Buddha

But it is no doubt Shakespeare who put it best: 'The fool doth think he is wise, but the wise man knows himself to be a fool.'

Still, there seems to be more to wisdom than mere 'negative knowledge', or else I could simply be super-skeptical about everything and count myself wise... Or, maybe wisdom consists in having very high epistemic standards, that is, in having a very high bar for believing something, and an even higher bar for calling that belief knowledge. But then we are back to a picture of wisdom as something like scientific knowledge.

In Plato's *Meno*, Socrates says that people of wisdom and virtue seem to be very poor at imparting those qualities: Themistocles was able to teach his son Cleophantus skills such as standing upright on horseback and shooting javelins, but no one ever credited Cleophantus with anything like his father's wisdom; and the same could also be said for Lysimachus and his son Aristides, Pericles and his sons Paralus and Xanthippus, and Thucydides and his sons Melesias and Stephanus. And if wisdom cannot be taught, not even by the wisest of Athenians, then it is not a kind of knowledge.

If wisdom cannot be taught, how, asks Meno, did good people come into existence? Socrates replies that right action is possible under guidance other than that of knowledge: a person who has knowledge about the way to Larisa may make a good guide, but a person who has only correct opinion about the way, but has never been and does not know, might make an equally good guide. Since wisdom cannot be taught, it cannot be knowledge; and if it cannot be knowledge, then it must be correct opinion—which explains why wise men such as Themistocles, Lysimachus, and Pericles were unable to impart their wisdom even unto their own sons. Wise people are no different from soothsayers, prophets, and poets, who say many true things when they are divinely inspired but have no real knowledge of what they are saying.

Aristotle gives us another important clue in the *Metaphysics*, when he says that wisdom is the understanding of causes. None of the senses are regarded as wisdom because, although they give the most authoritative knowledge of particulars, they are unable to discern the distal causes of anything. Similarly, we suppose artists to be wiser than people of mere experience because artists know the 'why' or the cause, and can therefore teach, whereas people of experience do not, and cannot. In other words, wisdom is the understanding of the right relations between things, which calls for more distant and removed perspectives, and maybe also the ability or willingness to shift between perspectives. In the *Tusculan Disputations*, Cicero cites as a paragon of wisdom the pre-Socratic philosopher Anaxagoras, who, upon being informed of the death of his son, said, 'I knew that I begot a mortal' [*Sciebam me genuisse mortalem*]. For Cicero, true sapience consists in preparing oneself for every eventuality so as never to be taken, or overtaken, by surprise. And it is true that wisdom, the understanding of causes and connexions, has forever been associated with both insight and foresight.

So wisdom is not so much a kind of knowledge as a way of seeing, or ways of seeing. When we take a few steps back, like when we stand under the shower or go on holiday, we begin to see the bigger picture. In everyday language use, 'wisdom' has two opposites: 'foolishness' and 'folly', which involve, respectively, lack and loss of perspective (both words derive from the Latin *follis*, 'bellows', 'bag'). For some thinkers, notably Robert Nozick, wisdom has a practical dimension in that it involves an understanding of the goals and values of life, the means of achieving those goals, the potential dangers to avoid, and so on. I agree, but I also think that all this naturally flows from perspective: if you have proper perspective, you cannot fail to understand the goals and values of life or indeed fail to act on that understanding. This chimes with Socrates' claim that nobody does wrong knowingly: people only do wrong because, from their limited perspective, it seems like the right or best thing for them to do. In the words of Jesus from the cross, 'Father, forgive them; for they know not what they do.'

In cultivating a broader perspective, it helps, of course, to be knowledgeable, but it also helps to be intelligent, reflective, open-minded, and disinterested—which is why we often seek out and pay for 'independent' advice. But above all it helps to be courageous, because the view from up there, though it can be exhilarating, and ultimately liberating, is at first terrifying, not least because it conflicts with so much of what we have been taught or programmed to think.

Courage, said Aristotle, is the first of the human qualities because it is the one which guarantees all the others.

How to cope with bad news

Your partner cheated or walked out on you. You've been fired. Your house has been burgled. You've been diagnosed with a life-changing condition. Bad news can leave us in a state of dread and despair. It seems like our whole world is falling apart, almost as if we're being driven into the ground. We fear the very worst and cannot get it out of our mind, or gut. Often, there are other emotions mangled in, like anger, guilt, despair, betrayal, and love. Bad news: we've all had it, and we're all going to get it.

So, how to cope? Here are three cognitive strategies that can help us to deal with bad news, and that can also help us to test the concept of wisdom as perspective.

1. *Contextualization.* Try to frame the bad news, to put it into its proper context. However bad it may feel, it is probably not the be-all and end-all of your life on this earth. Think about all the good things in your life, including those that have been and those that are yet to come. And think about all the strengths and resources—the friends, facilities, faculties—that you can still draw upon in your time of need. Try to imagine how things could be much, much worse—and how they actually are for

some people. Your house may have been burgled. Yes, you lost some valuables, and it's all such a huge hassle. But you still have your health, your job, your partner... Bad things are bound to hit us now and then, and it can only be a matter of time before they hit us again. In many cases, they are just the flip side of the good things that we enjoy. You got burgled, because you had a house and valuables. You lost a great relationship, because you had one in the first place. In that much, many a bad thing is no more than the removal of a good one.

2. *Negative visualization.* Now focus on the bad news itself. What's the worst that could happen, and is that really all that bad? Now that you've dealt with the worst, what's the best possible outcome? And what's the most likely outcome? Imagine that someone is threatening to sue you. The worst possible outcome is that you lose the case and suffer all the entailing cost, stress, and emotional and reputational hurt. Though it's unlikely, you might even do time in prison (it has happened to some, and a few did rather well out of it). But the most likely outcome is that you reach some sort of out-of-court settlement. And the best possible outcome is that you win the case, or better still, it gets dropped.

3. *Transformation.* Finally, try to transform your bad news into something positive, or at least into something that has positive aspects. Your bad news may represent a learning or strengthening experience, or act as a wake-up call, or force you to reassess your priorities. At the very least, it offers a window into the human condition and an opportunity to exercise dignity and self-control. Maybe you lost your job: time for a

holiday and a promotion, or a career change, or the freedom and fulfilment of self-employment. Maybe your partner cheated on you. Even so, you feel sure that he or she still loves you, that there is still something there. Perhaps you can even bring yourself to understand his or her motives. Yes, of course it's painful, but it may also be an opportunity to forgive, to build a closer intimacy, to re-launch your relationship—or to find an easier or more fulfilling one. You've been diagnosed with a serious medical condition. Though it's very bad news, it's also the chance to get the treatment and support that you need, to take control, to fight back, to look at life and your relationships from another, richer perspective.

In the words of John Milton: 'The mind is its own place, and in itself can make a heaven of hell, a hell of heaven.'

17

Inspiration

Think back to your favourite school teacher: for me, a French teacher who silently wept as he read to the class from a novel by Marguerite Duras. The teachers whom we hold dear in our hearts are not those who assiduously taught us the most facts, or fastidiously covered every bulleted point on the syllabus, but those who inspired us and opened us up to ourselves and to the world. But what is inspiration, and can it be cultivated?

The word 'inspiration' ultimately derives from the Greek for 'God-breathed' or 'divinely breathed into'. In Greek myth, inspiration is a gift of the muses, the nine daughters of Zeus and Mnemosyne ('Memory'), though it can also come from Apollo (*Apollon Mousagetēs*, 'Apollo Muse-leader'), Dionysus (god of wine), or Aphrodite (goddess of love). Homer famously invokes the muses in the very first line of the *Iliad*: 'Sing, O Muse, of the rage of Achilles, son of Peleus, that brought countless ills upon the Achaeans...' Similarly, the Church has long maintained that inspiration is a gift from the Holy Ghost, including the inspiration for the Bible itself: 'For the prophecy came not in old time by the will of man: but holy men of God spake as they were moved by the Holy Ghost' (2 Peter 1:21).

The Oxford English Dictionary defines inspiration as 'a breathing in or infusion of some idea, purpose, etc. into the mind; the suggestion, awakening, or creation of some feeling or impulse, especially of an exalted kind'. Going with this, there appear to be two aspects to inspiration: some kind of vision, along with some kind of positive energy that derives from and drives towards that vision. Inspiration is often confused with 'motivation' and 'creativity'. Motivation aims at some sort of external reward, whereas inspiration comes from within and is very much its own reward. Although inspiration is associated with creative insight, creativity also involves the realization of that insight—which requires opportunity, means, and, above all, effort. In the words of Thomas Edison, genius is 1 percent inspiration, 99 percent perspiration—although you may not get started, or get very far, without that initial 1 percent.

Other than creativity, inspiration has been linked with enthusiasm, optimism, and self-esteem. Inspiration need not be all artistic and highfalutin: I often feel inspired to garden or cook, to plant out some bulbs for next spring or make use of a seasonal ingredient. These inspired tasks feel very different from, say, writing a letter of complaint or filing my tax return. If I could be paid to do what inspires me, and pay others to do what does not, I should be a very happy man, and probably a very successful one too.

Despite its importance to both society and the individual, our system of education leaves very little place for inspiration—perhaps because, like wisdom and virtue, it cannot easily be taught but only ever... inspired. Unfortunately, a person who has never been inspired is unlikely to inspire others. That is a great shame. The best education consists not in being taught, but in being inspired; and if I could, I would rather inspire a single person than teach a thousand.

But where does inspiration come from in the first place? In Plato's *Ion*, Socrates likens inspiration to a divine power, and this divine power to a magnetic stone that can not only move iron rings, but also magnetize the iron rings so that they too can do the same. This leads to a long chain of iron rings, with each ring's energy ultimately derived from that of the original magnetic stone. If a poet is any good, this is not because she has read every book on her subject with an underlining pen, but because she is divinely inspired, divinely possessed:

> *For the poet is a light and winged and holy thing, and there is no invention in him until he has been inspired and is out of his senses, and the mind is no longer in him: when he has not attained to this state, he is powerless and is unable to utter his oracles.*

Socrates compares inspired poets to the Bacchic maidens, who are out of their minds when they draw honey and milk from the rivers, when others cannot even draw milk. He asks Ion, a rhapsode (reciter of poetry), whether, when he recites Homer, he does not get beside himself, whether his soul does not believe that it is witnessing the actions of which he sings. Ion replies that when he sings of something sad, his eyes are full of tears, and when he sings of something frightening, his hairs stand on end, such that he is no longer in his right mind.

Socrates says that this is precisely the effect that a rhapsode has on his audience: the muse inspires the poet, the poet the rhapsode, and the rhapsode his audience, which is the last of the iron rings in the divine chain.

In Plato's *Phaedrus*, Socrates argues that madness, as well as being an illness, can be the source of our greatest blessings (Chapter 15). There are, he continues, four kinds of inspired madness: prophecy, from Apollo; holy prayers and mystic rites, from Dionysus; poetry, from the muses; and love, from Aphrodite and Eros.

> *But if a man comes to the door of poetry untouched by the madness of the muses, believing that technique alone will make him a good poet, he and his sane companions never reach perfection, but are utterly eclipsed by the performances of the inspired madman.*

All human beings, says Socrates, are able to recollect universals, such as perfect goodness and perfect beauty, and must therefore have seen them in some other life or other world. The souls that came closest to the universals, and that experienced them most profoundly, are reincarnated into philosophers, artists, and true lovers. As the universals are still strongly imprinted onto their minds, they are completely absorbed in ideas about them and forget all about earthly interests. Humdrum people think that they are mad, but the truth is that they are divinely inspired and in love with goodness and beauty. In the twentieth century, Jung echoed Plato, arguing that the artist is one who can reach beyond individual experience to access our genetic memory, that is, the memory, such as the memory for language, that is already present in us at birth. Recall that, in Greek myth, Memory/Mnemosyne is the mother of the muses.

The idea that 'madness' is closely allied with inspiration and revelation is an old and recurring one. In *Of Peace of Mind*, Seneca concludes that 'there is no great genius without a tincture of madness' [*nullum magnum ingenium sine mixtuae dementiae fuit*], a maxim which he attributes to Aristotle, and which is also echoed in Cicero. For Shakespeare, 'the lunatic, the lover, and the poet are of imagination all compact.' And for Dryden, 'great wits are sure to madness near allied, and thin partitions do their bounds divide.' As I argued in a book called *The Meaning of Madness*, our reservoir of madness, often perceived as the polar opposite of reason, is in fact a precious resource that we can learn to tap into.

For the writer André Gide:

> *The most beautiful things are those that are whispered by madness and written down by reason. We must steer a course between the two, close to madness in our dreams, but close to reason in our writing.*

In sum, it seems that inspiration amounts to some sort of alignment or channelling of primal energies, which cannot quite be summoned or relied upon.

Nonetheless, here are seven simple strategies for inspiring inspiration:

1. *Wake up when your body tells you to.* No one has ever been tired and inspired at the same time. To make matters worse, having our sleep interrupted by an alarm clock or other stimulus can leave us feeling groggy and grouchy, as though we had 'woken up on the wrong foot'.

2. *Complete your dreams.* REM sleep, which is associated with dreaming, is richest just before *natural* awakening. Dreaming serves a number of critical functions, such as assimilating experiences, processing emotions, and enhancing problem solving and creativity. In fact, the brain can be more active during REM sleep than during wakefulness. Many great works of art have been inspired by dreams, including Paul McCartney's *Let it Be*, Salvador Dali's *Persistence of Memory*, and several of Edgar Allan Poe's poems and short stories. In addition, awaking after REM is associated with feeling refreshed, and people who wake up after REM perform better on tasks like anagrams and creative problem solving.

3. *Eliminate distractions, especially the tedious ones.* Clear your diary, remove yourself from the world, take plenty of time over everything. You want to give your mind plenty of spare capacity. You want it to roam, to freewheel. Before going to bed, I check my calendar for the next day's engagements, and am never happier than when I see a blank page. Don't worry or feel guilty, the roof won't fall down, the sun won't drop out of the sky. Many people are unable to let their minds wander off the beaten path for fear of the monsters that may be lurking in the undergrowth. If you meet a monster, take the chance to say 'hello'.

4. *Don't rush things.* If you try to force inspiration, you will strangle it. You will achieve much less overall, if not also in quantity then at least in quality. There may be 'on' days and 'off' days, or even 'on' hours and 'off' hours. If you don't feel inspired, that's fine, go out and replenish yourself. Your boss may disagree, but it's probably the most productive thing you could do. If you can, try not to have a boss.

5. *Be curious.* John Locke suggested that inspiration amounts to a somewhat random association of ideas and sudden unison of thought. If something, anything, catches your interest, try to follow it through. Nothing is too small or irrelevant. Read books, watch documentaries, visit museums and exhibitions, walk in gardens and nature, interact with inspired and inspiring people… Feed your unconscious.

6. *Break the routine.* Sometimes it can help to give the mind a bit of a shake. Try new things that take you out of your comfort zone. Modify your routine or surroundings. Better still, go travelling, especially to places that are unfamiliar and disorienting, such as a temple in India or Japan, or a hippy farm in the Uruguayan pampas (I tried that and drove off after just four hours).

7 *Make a start.* When I write an article or chapter, I make a start and come back to it whenever I next feel inspired. The minute I start flagging, I stop and do something else, and, hopefully, while I do that, the next paragraph or section enters my mind. Some pieces I write over three or four days, others over three or four weeks—but hardly ever do I write a piece in a single sitting or even a single day. When I write a book,

the first half seems to take forever, while the second half gets completed in a fraction of the time. Small accomplishments are important in that they boost confidence and free the mind to move on, establishing a kind of creative momentum.

If you learn to work with and never against your nature, things will get done as if by themselves.

18

Insight

'Insight' is sometimes used to mean something like 'self-awareness', including awareness of our thought processes, beliefs, desires, emotions, and so on, and how they might relate to one another and to truth or expediency.

Of course, self-awareness comes by degrees. Owing to chemical receptors in their tendrils, vining plants know not to coil around themselves, and in this respect can be said to have awareness of self and not-self. Children begin to develop reflective self-awareness at around eighteen months of age, enabling them to recognize themselves in pictures and mirrors.

But insight is also used to mean something like 'penetrating discernment', especially in cases when a solution to a previously intractable problem suddenly presents itself—and it is on this particular meaning of the word that I want to concentrate.

Such 'aha moments', epitomized by Archimedes' cry of *Eureka! Eureka!* [Greek, 'I found it! I found it!], involve seeing something familiar in a new light or context, particularly a brighter or broader one, leading to a novel perspective and positive emotions such as joy, enthusiasm, and confidence. It is said that, upon sinking into his bath, Archimedes noticed the water level rising and suddenly understood that the volume of water displaced corresponded to the volume of the parts of his body that had been submerged. Lesser examples of aha moments include suddenly understanding a joke, or suddenly perceiving the other aspect of a reversal image such as the duck-rabbit optical illusion (Figure 6). Aha moments result primarily from unconscious and automatic processes, and—you will have noticed—our eyes naturally tend, when working on insight problems, to look away from visual stimuli.

Aha moments can be compared to and distinguished from uh-oh moments, in which we suddenly become aware of an unforeseen problem, and d'oh moments, popularized by Homer Simpson, when an unforeseen problem hits us and/or we have a flash of insight into our lack of insight.

'Thinking out of the box' is a significant cognitive achievement. Once we have understood something in one way, it is very difficult to apprehend it in any other way, even in the face of strong contradictory evidence. In *When Prophecy Fails*, Leon Festinger discusses his experience of infiltrating a UFO doomsday cult whose leader had prophesied the end of the world. When the end of the world predictably failed to materialize, most of the cult members dealt with the dissonance that arose from the cognitions 'the leader said that the world would end' and 'the world did not end' not by abandoning the cult or its leader, as you might expect, but by introducing the rationalization that the world had been saved by the strength of their faith!

Insight

Figure 6: The duck-rabbit ambiguous image.

Very often, to see something in a different light also means to see ourselves and the whole world in that new light, which can threaten and undermine our sense of self. It is more a matter of the emotions than of reason, which explains why even eminent scientists can struggle with perceptual shifts. As discussed in Chapter 13 on the problems of science, paradigm shifts occur less by a triumph of reason, which serves mostly to justify pre-existing beliefs, than by the rising up of a new generation to replace the last.

Worse still, strong contradictory evidence or attempts to convince us otherwise can, in fact, be counterproductive and entrench our existing beliefs—which is why as a psychiatrist I rarely challenge my patients, or indeed anyone, directly. But you don't have to take my word for it: in one recent study, supplying 'corrective information' to people with serious concerns about the adverse effects of the flu jab actually made them *less* willing to receive it. This more than substantiates the German proverb, *Gib niemals ungefragt einen Rat. Der Weise braucht ihn nicht, der Narr nimmt ihn nicht an.* [Never give advice unless asked. The wise man won't need it, the fool won't heed it.]

So, short of dissolving our egos like a zen master, what can we do to improve our cognitive flexibility? Of course, it helps to have the tools of thought, including language fluency and multiple frames of reference as given by knowledge and experience. But much more important is to develop that first sense of insight—namely, insight as self-awareness.

On a more day-to-day basis, we need to create the time and conditions for thoughts to connect. My own associative thinking is much more active when I'm both well-rested and at rest, for example, standing under the shower or ambling in the park. Jack Welch, as Chairman and CEO of General Electric, spent an hour each day in what he called 'looking out of the window time'. August Kekulé claimed to have discovered the ring structure of the benzene molecule while daydreaming about a snake biting its own tail.

Time is a very strange thing and not at all linear: sometimes, the best way of using it is to waste it.

19

Emotion

As discussed in Chapter 9, the intricacies of human affairs often lead to a paralysis of reason. That we are much better at making decisions than machines has much to do with our emotions, which define the parameters of any particular deliberation and carry to conscious attention only a small selection of all the available facts and alternatives. Our emotions also motivate us, and people with a diminished capacity for emotion—whether from brain injury, severe depression, or another mental disorder—find it especially hard to make decisions let alone act upon them.

With the decline of religion and traditional social structures, our emotions have come to assume an increasingly dominant role in our lives. It has forever been said that man is ruled by his emotions, but this today is truer than ever. Much more than reason or tradition, it is our emotions that determine our choice of profession, partner, and politics, and our relation to money, sex, and God. Yet, remarkably, the emotions are utterly neglected by our system of education, leading to millions of mis-lived lives. Nothing can make us feel more alive, or more human, than our emotions, or hurt us more. To control our emotions is to control ourselves, and to control ourselves is to control our destiny.

But what exactly is an emotion? The answer is not entirely clear. 'Emotion' is a relatively recent term and there are languages that do not carry an equivalent. Historically, people spoke not of emotions but of passions. The passions encompass, or encompassed, not only the emotions, but also pleasure, pain, and desire. 'Passion', like 'passivity', derives from the Latin *patere*, 'to suffer'. It has often seemed that the passive passions are not within our control, and today the term has come to refer to a powerful or compelling feeling or desire, especially love or lust, while also retaining the more restricted mediæval meaning of the suffering of Christ on the Cross and the martyrdom of the saints. The notion of passivity is retained in 'emotion', which derives from the Latin *emovere*, 'to move out, remove, agitate'. To *suffer* an emotion is to be acted upon, to be disturbed, and to be afflicted.

A long line of thinkers have opposed the 'animal' passions to calm and God-like reason, with various authorities from the Stoics to Spinoza going so far as to advocate *apatheia*, that is, the suppression of feeling, emotion, and concern. Unfortunately, this historical privileging of reason has led not so much to the suppression of feeling as to its near complete disregard. Today, the emotions are so neglected that most people are oblivious to the deep currents that move them, hold them back, and lead them astray.

If I say, 'I am grateful', I could mean one of three things: that I am currently feeling grateful for something, that I generally feel grateful for that thing, or that I am a grateful kind of person. Similarly, if I say, 'I am proud', I could mean that I am currently feeling proud about something, that I generally feel proud about that thing, or that I am a proud kind of person. Let us call the first instance (currently feeling proud about something) an emotional experience, the second instance (generally feeling proud about that thing) an emotion or sentiment, and the third instance (being a proud kind of person) a trait.

It is very common to confuse or amalgamate these three instances, especially the first and the second. But whereas an emotional experience is brief and episodic, an emotion—which may or may not result from accreted emotional experiences—can endure for many years, and, in that time, predispose to a variety of emotional experiences, as well as thoughts, beliefs, desires, and actions. For instance, love can give rise not only to amorous feelings, but also to joy, grief, rage, longing, and jealousy, among others.

Similarly, it is very common to confuse emotions and feelings. An emotional experience, by virtue of being a conscious experience, is necessarily a feeling, as are physical sensations such as hunger or pain (although not all conscious experiences are also feelings, not, for example, believing or seeing, presumably because they lack a somatic or bodily dimension). By contrast, an emotion, being in some sense latent, can only ever be felt, *sensu stricto*, through the emotional experiences that it gives rise to, even though it might also be discovered through its associated thoughts, beliefs, desires, and actions. Despite their various manifestations, emotions need not themselves be conscious, and some emotions, such as hating one's mother or being in love with one's best friend, might only be uncovered, let alone admitted, after several years in psychotherapy.

If an emotion remains unconscious, this is often by repression or some other form of self-deception (Chapter 5). Of course, self-deception can also take place at the level of an emotional experience, commonly by misattributing the type or intensity of the emotional experience or misattributing its object or cause. Thus, envy is often construed as indignation, and *Schadenfreude* (the pleasure derived from the misfortune of others) as sympathy. Fear of ghosts or 'the dark' is almost certainly fear of death, since people who have come to terms with death are hardly frightened of such phantasms. Beyond this, it could be argued that even the purest of emotions is inherently self-deceptive in so far as it lends weight in our experience to one thing, or some things, over others. In that much, emotions are not objective or neutral perceptions, but subjective 'ways of seeing' that reflect our individual needs and concerns.

Having distinguished between emotions, emotional experiences, and feelings, I ought to say something about traits. A trait is a disposition to have certain emotions and emotional experiences. Traits also encompass certain characteristic thoughts, beliefs, desires, and actions, and can in turn be shaped by these elements. Traits are often named for their predominant emotion and classified as either virtue or vice, for example, humility (virtue), gratitude (virtue), and greed (vice). That said, a number of old-fashioned virtues do not involve any one predominant emotion but instead *control* of the emotions, for example, fortitude, prudence, and temperance.

One can also distinguish between temperamental traits and character traits. Temperamental traits are innate and cannot altogether be altered, whereas character traits are more open, or less closed, to shaping. 'Character' derives from the Greek *charaktêr*, which refers to the mark impressed upon a coin, and character traits can become so ingrained as to imprint themselves onto our physical features. As Coco Chanel once quipped, 'Nature gives you the face you have at twenty. Life shapes the face you have at thirty. But at fifty you get the face you deserve.'

The emotions are very varied. For instance, they can be non-moral or moral, non-reflexive or reflexive (about the self, such as embarrassment or guilt), and first-order or second-order (about another emotion, such as shame at my fear). They can also be positive, negative, or, as with anger or nostalgia, both negative and positive. The only emotion that does not appear to carry a consistent valence is surprise, which can be positive, negative, or mixed—although, of course, every individual instance of surprise is either one or another.

An emotion may be positive or negative by virtue of being pleasant or unpleasant, pleasant emotions being reactions to those things that have tended to sustain and validate us in the course of our evolutionary history, and unpleasant emotions to those things that have tended to undermine us. An important implication is that our emotions may not be entirely adapted to modern life. In particular, our emotions tend to short-term bias, leading to the hyperbolic discounting of long-term pleasure. In the distant past, this short-term bias increased our chances of survival and reproduction, but with increased life expectancies etc. it has turned into a significant liability. Negative emotions, negative though they may be, can become pleasant if their object is a mere simulacrum, which is why people pay good money to watch horror films and ride rollercoasters, to speak nothing of sadomasochism.

Some emotions, such as humility or nostalgia, are clearly more complex and nuanced than others, for which reason they are not usually attributed to infants and animals. The concept of 'basic' or 'primary' emotions dates back at least to the *Book of Rites*, a first-century Chinese encyclopædia that identifies seven 'feelings of men': joy, anger, sadness, fear, love, disliking, and liking. In the twentieth century, Paul Ekman identified six basic emotions (anger, disgust, fear, happiness, sadness, and surprise) and Robert Plutchik eight, which he grouped into four oppositional pairs (joy-sadness, anger-fear, trust-distrust, surprise-anticipation).

Basic emotions evolved in response to the ecological challenges faced by our remote ancestors and are so primitive as to be 'hardwired', with each basic emotion corresponding to a distinct and dedicated neurological circuit. Being hardwired, basic emotions (or 'affect programs') are innate and universal, automatic, and fast, and trigger behaviour with a high survival value. While holidaying on the tropical island of Mauritius, I opened a cutlery drawer on a large lizard, which, of course,

I had not been expecting to find among the forks and knives. As the critter darted off into the blackness behind the drawer, I unthinkingly jumped back and slammed the drawer shut. Having done this, I suddenly became aware of feeling hot and alert and primed for further action. This basic fear response is so primitive that even the lizard seemed to share in it, and so automatic as to be 'cognitively impenetrable', that is, unconscious and uncontrollable, and more akin to a reflex or reaction than a deliberate action.

One hypothesis is that basic emotions can function as building blocks, with more complex emotions being blends of basic ones. For instance, contempt might amount to a blend of anger and disgust. In 1980, Robert Plutchik constructed a wheel-like diagram of emotions with eight basic emotions, plus eight derivative emotions each composed of two basic ones (Figure 7). However, many complex emotions cannot be deconstructed into more basic ones, and the theory does not explain why infants and animals do not share (or appear to share) in complex emotions. Instead, it could be that complex emotions are an amalgam of basic emotions and cognitions, with certain combinations being sufficiently common or important to be named in language. Thus, frustration might amount to anger combined with the thought or belief that 'nothing can be done'. But again, many complex emotions resist such analysis. What's more, 'basic' emotions can themselves result from quite complex cognitions, for instance, Tim's panic upon realizing—or simply believing—that he has slept through an important exam.

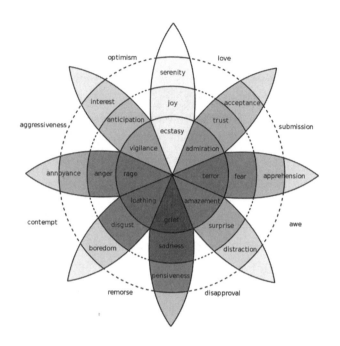

Figure 7: Plutchik's wheel.

Although basic emotions have been compared to programs, it does seem that their potential objects are open to cultural conditioning. If poor Tim fears having missed his exam, this is in large part because of the value that his culture and micro-culture attach to academic success. With more complex emotions, it is the emotion itself (rather than its potential object) that is culturally shaped and constructed. *Schadenfreude* is not common to all peoples in all times. And neither is romantic love, which seems to have emerged in tandem with the novel. In *Madame Bovary*, itself a novel, Gustave Flaubert tells us that Emma Bovary only found out about romantic love through 'the refuse of old lending libraries'. These books, he continues,

> ...were all about love and lovers, damsels in distress swooning in lonely lodges, postillions slaughtered all along the road, horses ridden to death on every page, gloomy forests, troubles of the heart, vows, sobs, tears, kisses, rowing-boats in the moonlight, nightingales in the grove, gentlemen brave as lions and gentle as lambs, too virtuous to be true, invariably well-dressed, and weeping like fountains.

Cultural conditioning also extends to the expression of emotion, with some expressions being as localized as dialects. At the other end of the spectrum, the facial expressions of basic emotions are so resistant to cultural conditioning as to be universally shared and recognized. Indeed, some even extend to certain animals, enabling us to feel great empathy with our canine friends among others. Expressions of emotion are very varied, and include smiling, frowning, laughing, crying, wailing, jumping back, jumping up, covering the brow, covering the face, kissing, caressing, dancing... Even actions that are not primarily to do with emotional expression can become suffused with emotion, for instance, closing the door (softly or with a slam) or pulling out a pen from our coat pocket.

Some if not most expressions of emotion have functional purposes, for instance, baring the teeth and clenching the fists can serve to intimidate or prepare for attack. In addition, all expressions of emotion serve to signal the emotion—and by extension the evaluation to which the emotion corresponds—to others, forming a system of communication that far antedates language in evolution. In signalling an emotion or evaluation, expressions of emotion aim to inspire the same or a countervailing emotion in others—commonly admiration, sympathy, curiosity, amusement, fear, guilt, or shame.

All this implies that others are competent at reading expressions of emotion. Our ability to interpret expressions of emotion is automatic and unreflective, even with emotions that we ourselves have never experienced, or only partially. It rests on the assumption that others share in a psychology that is similar to our own, which is why we exercise caution when dealing with people of a different culture, generation, or social class. As the expressions of basic emotions are universally shared, this caution need only extend to more complex emotions—something which we intuitively understand without ever having given it any conscious thought.

Varied though they are, all emotions are associated with a certain felt quality. For instance, fear is associated with a physiological response involving, among others, a rise in heart rate, increased muscle tension, perspiration, and piloerection (goose bumps), not to mention expressions of fear such as stiffening of the body, cessation of movement, widening of the eyes, and flaring of the nostrils. William James argued that, without such bodily modifications, an emotion would be reduced to 'a cold and neutral state of intellectual perception'. According to the James-Lange theory, an emotion amounts to no more than the experience of these bodily modifications.

Thus, in the words of James, 'we feel sorry because we cry, angry because we strike, afraid because we tremble, and [it is] not that we cry, strike, or tremble, because we are sorry, angry, or fearful, as the case may be.'

Unfortunately, this does seem to be putting the cart before the horse. I am not afraid because I tremble; rather, I tremble because I am afraid. My trembling is not the cause, but a part, of my fear. Even if there could be enough distinct combinations of bodily modifications to represent every nuanced emotion, it is not at all clear that every emotion need involve bodily modifications, or, conversely, that bodily modifications (for example, in exercise or illness) need give rise to an emotion. People with high-level spinal cord lesions do not have a reduced range of emotions, and experimental subjects injected with adrenaline (epinephrine) interpret their arousal differently depending on the situation in which they happen to find themselves.

And yet there is a sense in which the James-Lange theory gets it right. Emotional tears (as opposed to reflexive tears such as those from chopping onions) serve a number of social functions such as emphasizing the depth and sincerity of our emotions, and attracting attention, sympathy, and support in times of danger, distress, or need. But they also serve an important psychological function, which is to tell us that a particular problem or situation actually means a lot to us, and that we need to make the time and effort to address or at least process it—opening out, in due course, on a healthier attitude or clearer perspective. As markers of strong emotion, emotional tears signal moments of existential importance in our lives, from sharing a first kiss to grieving the loss of our partner. Our tears reveal us to ourselves, and, in so doing, make us more like ourselves—which is why we should be encouraging and interpreting them rather than holding them back.

More broadly, an emotion can give us privileged access to an evaluative stance, with the name of the emotion being shorthand for that evaluative stance. But it can sometimes be difficult to put a name on an emotion or emotional experience, let alone fully understand it. First, there are far more emotions than have been named in language. Second, emotions are often blended with other emotions or dominated by some other mental state—for instance, fear is often dominated by the desire or impulse to escape, and only fully felt retrospectively. And third, certain emotions are simply too uncomfortable to rest upon, not least because doing so could give rise to further uncomfortable emotions.

Our emotions not only reflect and reveal our values, they also enable us to refine them. It is possible to have an emotion about an emotion, and to revise the first-order emotion according to the second-order emotion or emotions. Moreover, some of our emotions can feel clear and transparent, while others are more hazy or equivocal. For instance, our love for truth or justice is experienced as profound and authentic, whereas our resentment or disdain for someone of higher virtue or accomplishment rings hollow and leaves us uneasy.

If our values are distorted, so are our emotions, leading us to feel and act against our best or long-term interests. Indeed, a single stray emotion or emotional experience can lay waste to the best plans of half a lifetime. It is in this sense that the emotions are said to be 'irrational', but, of course, poor feeling is no more irrational than poor thinking. Thinking and feeling are closely interrelated, so much so that it is possible to use our feelings to verify our thinking. This checking function underlies my basic political principle: if something, whether right- or left-wing, is driven by love and solidarity, it is right; but if it is driven by hate and fear, it is wrong. By the use of feeling, it really can be as simple as that.

In the dance between thinking and feeling, feeling does the leading, and is the better dancer—whence Hume's aphorism that 'reason is, and ought only to be the slave of the passions'. Poor feeling hijacks thinking for self-deception (Chapter 5): to hide harsh truths, evade responsibility, avoid action, and, as the existentialists might put it, flee from freedom. Thus, poor feeling is a kind of moral failing, indeed, the deepest kind, and virtue principally consists in correcting and refining our emotions and the values that they reflect.

To feel the right thing is to do the right thing, without any particular need for conscious thought or effort. Conversely, repeated right action can eventually lead to right feeling. Aristotle, the father of logic and master reasoner, held that, in most people, right acting and right feeling, or virtue, is not the product of rational deliberation but merely a matter of habit. In the *Nicomachean Ethics*, he concedes that,

> *...if arguments were in themselves enough to make men good, they would justly, as Theognis says, have won very great rewards, and such rewards should have been provided; but as things are, while they seem to have power to encourage and stimulate the generous-minded among our youths, and to make a character which is gently born, and a true lover of what is noble, ready to be possessed by virtue, they are not able to encourage the many to nobility and goodness.*

At the end of the *Nicomachean Ethics*, Aristotle says that arguments and teaching can only take hold in a soul that is good by nature, or that has been cultivated by good habits, and that good habits are the product of good laws. So he writes his next book, the *Politics*.

The psychology of snobbery

Let's look more closely at the relationship between reason, emotion, and action through an analysis of snobbery, which is running rampant in our divided society.

It is sometimes said that the word 'snob' originated from the Latin *sine nobilitate* ['without nobility'], used in abbreviated form—*s.nob*—on lists of names by Cambridge colleges, passenger ships etc. to distinguish between titled and non-titled persons. In fact, 'snob' was first recorded in the late eighteenth century as a term for a shoemaker or his apprentice, though it is true that Cambridge students came to apply it to those outside the university. By the early nineteenth century, 'snob' had come to mean something like 'a person who lacks breeding', and then, as social structures became more fluid, 'a social climber'.

Today, a snob is someone who:
- Accords exaggerated importance to one or more superficial attributes such as wealth, social status, beauty, or academic credentials,
- Perceives people with those attributes to be of higher human worth,
- Lays claim to those attributes for him- or her-self, often unduly, and,
- Denigrates all those who lack those attributes.

So there are three main aspects to snobbery: exaggerating the importance of certain attributes, laying claim to those attributes, and, last but not least, denigrating those who lack them. 'I'm not a snob,' said Simon Le Bon, 'Ask anybody. Well, anybody who matters.'

Snobbery is not simply a matter of discernment, however expensive or refined our tastes may be: a so-called wine snob, who enjoys and even insists on good wine, may or may not be an actual snob, depending on the degree of his or her prejudice (from the Latin *praeiudicium*, 'prior judgement'). Some young sommeliers, immersed as they are in the world of wine, can come to place undue value on wine knowledge, to the point of deprecating their own, less informed, patrons—a phenomenon that has been dubbed 'sommelier syndrome'.

Aside from its obvious unpleasantness to others, snobbery tends to undermine the snob, his achievements, and the interests and institutions that he represents. As a UK Conservative Party parliamentary candidate in 2006, Jacob Rees-Mogg did himself and his party no favours when he compared people who had not studied at Oxford or Cambridge to 'potted plants'.

Snobbery betrays rigidity of thinking and therefore poor judgement, as with those British aristocrats who, despite their expensive educations, came to admire Hitler's autocratic style of government. The thinking, in so far as it can be called thinking, is not just rigid but warped. The snob pigeonholes people according to superficial criteria such as their profession, their house, or, especially in England, their accent, and, on that basis, either regards or disregards them: like the wine snob who will only drink certain labels, he often passes over real value, quality, or originality. As a companion, the snob is an endless bore, constantly detracting from the rich texture of life and quite unable to marvel at anything except through himself.

Closely related to snobbery, and presenting some of the same pitfalls, is 'inverse snobbery'. Inverse snobbery is the disdain for those same traits that the snob might hold in high regard, combined with admiration, whether real or feigned, for the popular, the ordinary, and the commonplace. Inverse snobbery can be understood, in large part, as an ego defence against the status claims of others; and it is possible, indeed common, to be both a snob and an inverse snob.

But what about snobbery itself? Like inverse snobbery, snobbery can be interpreted as a symptom of social insecurity. Social insecurity may be rooted in childhood experiences, especially feelings of shame at being different, or an early sense of privilege or entitlement that cannot be realized in later life. Or it may be the simple result of rapid social change. With Brexit in the UK and the election of Donald Trump in the US, the ebbing of power from traditional, cultured elites has led, on all sides, to a surge in both snobbery and inverse snobbery.

In a similar vein, some snobbery may represent a reaction to an increasingly egalitarian society, reflecting a deeply ingrained human instinct that some people are better than others, that these people are more fit to rule, and that their rule tends to yield better outcomes—though, of course, one need not be a snob to share in such ideas. In that much, snobbery can serve as a mechanism of class surveillance and control—as can, paradoxically, inverse snobbery—serving to entrench social hierarchies.

Finally, at an extreme, snobbery may be a manifestation of narcissistic personality disorder or broader psychopathy... which helpfully points to its antidote, namely, the opposite of psychopathy, or empathy. Snobbery, said Hugh Kingsmill, 'is the desire for what divides men, and the inability to value what unites them.'

Reason is but the slave of the passions: employing empathy to alleviate snobbery is, I think, an excellent example of better feeling opening up onto better thinking and better acting.

*Significant sections of the first part of this chapter are adapted from the introduction to *Heaven and Hell: The Psychology of the Emotions* (2015).

20

Music

The oldest musical instruments to have been found—flutes made from bird bone and mammoth ivory—are more than 42,000 years old; and it has been argued that, by fostering social cohesion, music—from the Greek, 'the art of the muses'—could have helped our species outcompete the Neanderthals. Remember that next time you stand up to your national anthem.

In the Bible, David played on his harp to make King Saul feel better: 'And it came to pass, when the evil spirit from God was upon Saul, that David took an harp, and played with his hand: so Saul was refreshed, and was well, and the evil spirit departed from him.'

The oral works ascribed to Homer would not have survived had they not been set to music and sung. By his song, the lyric poet Thaletas brought civic harmony to Ancient Sparta and is even credited with ending the plague in that city. The Pythagoreans recited poetry, sang hymns to Apollo (the god of arts and music), and played on the lyre to cure illnesses of body and soul. In the *Republic*, Plato says that the education of the guardians of the state should consist of gymnastics for the body and music for the soul, and that, once set, the curriculum should not be changed: '...when modes of music change, of the State always change with them.' Aristotle concludes the *Politics* with, of all things, a discussion of music:

> *Since then music is a pleasure, and virtue consists in rejoicing and loving and hating aright, there is clearly nothing which we are so much concerned to acquire and to cultivate as the power of forming right judgements, and of taking delight in good dispositions and noble actions. Rhythm and melody supply imitations of anger and gentleness, and also of courage and temperance, and all the qualities contrary to these, and of the other qualities of character, which hardly fall short of the actual affections...*

In the tenth century, the Islamic thinker Al-Farabi wrote a treatise, *Meanings of the Intellect*, in which he discussed music therapy. Modern music therapy took form in the aftermath of the Second World War, when staff in veteran hospitals noticed that music could benefit their patients in ways that standard treatments could not. In 1959, American composer and pianist Paul Nordoff and British special education teacher Clive Robbins developed a form of collaborative music-making to engage vulnerable and isolated children, helping them to develop in the cognitive, behavioural, and social domains. Today, Nordoff Robbins is the largest music therapy charity in the UK.

Does music therapy work? And if so, how? Music boosts levels of dopamine, a feel-good chemical messenger in the brain. Many people use music to power through a workout. Beyond distracting from discomfort, music triggers the release of opioid hormones that relieve physical and psychological pain. But forget the workout, just dance to the music! Dancing is the best exercise because it involves start-stop movement in all directions and engages the mind on multiple levels. Music also boosts the immune system, notably by increasing antibodies and decreasing stress hormones. Techno and heavy metal aside, music lowers heart rate and blood pressure, and even reduces recovery time following a heart episode or surgery.

From a more psychological perspective, music therapy alleviates symptoms of anxiety and depression and improves social and occupational functioning. Aside from the biological benefits such as increased dopamine and decreased stress hormones that I've just discussed, music can help us to recognize, express, and process complex or painful emotions. It elevates these emotions and gives them a sense of legitimacy, of context and perspective, of order, beauty, and meaning. For Schopenhauer, the progression of musical notes, especially the melody on top, mirrors the progress of our own inner striving. Music is the school and the hospital of the emotions. It replicates the structures of emotions without however furnishing their contents, enabling us to feel the emotions without feeling or fearing the pain that they are normally associated with.

I don't think that music has to sound uplifting to be uplifting, so long as it helps us to work with our emotions. In the *Poetics*, Aristotle compared the purifying or cleansing effects of tragedy on the mind of the spectator to the effect of a cathartic on the body, and called this purging of the emotions *catharsis*. In that much, tragedy is more comforting, because more real, more faithful, than comedy, which so often rings hollow.

The benefit of music extends beyond depression and anxiety to psychosis, autism, and dementia. I've noticed that when people lose the faculty of speech through brain damage (most commonly dementia or stroke), the ability to sing is often preserved—along with, of all things, the ability to swear. In dementia, music can help with cognitive deficits, agitation, and social functioning. It assists the encoding of memories, and can, in turn, evoke vivid memories. In acquired brain injury, it can assist with the recovery of motor skills, and, through song, lend a voice to people who have lost the faculty of speech. At the other end of life, music played during pregnancy has been linked, in the newborn, to better motor and cognitive skills, faster development of language, and so on.

I remember as a teenager, lying in the blackness of the night and listening to Beethoven on my (now antiquated) discman. I could swear that these experiences completely transformed the makeup of my mind.

21

Imagination

Einstein held that imagination is more important than knowledge: 'I am enough of the artist to draw freely upon my imagination. Knowledge is limited. Imagination encircles the world.'

I define imagination as the faculty of the mind that forms and manipulates images, propositions, concepts, emotions, and sensations above and beyond, and sometimes independently of, incoming stimuli, to open up the realms of the abstract, the figurative, the possible, the hypothetical, and the paradigmatic or universal.

Imagination comes in many forms and by many degrees, ranging from scientific reasoning to musical appreciation; and overlaps with a number of other cognitive constructs including belief, desire, emotion, memory, supposition, and fantasy. Belief, like perception, aims at according with reality, while desire aims at altering reality. Like belief, emotion also aims at according with reality, but more particularly at reflecting the significance of its object, or class of object, for the subject—an aspect that it shares with many forms of imagination. Like imagination, memory can involve remote imagery. But unlike imagination, memory is (or aims to be) rooted in reality and serves primarily to frame belief and guide moment-by-moment action. Memories are often more vivid than imaginings, which are, in turn, more vivid that mere suppositions. Suppositions tend to be cold and cognitive, and lacking in the emotional and existential dimensions of imagination, and in its vividness. Finally, fantasy may be understood as a type of imagination, namely, imagination for the improbable.

I say the improbable rather than the impossible, because there is a theory that, just as perception justifies beliefs about actuality, so imagination justifies beliefs about possibility (or at least, metaphysical as opposed to natural possibility). To quote Hume, 'it is an established maxim in metaphysics, that whatever the mind clearly conceives, includes the idea of possible existence, or in other words, that nothing we imagine is absolutely impossible.' Could ghosts, the devil, time travel, and other imaginary things really be possible? I think inconceivability may be a better guide to impossibility than conceivability to possibility. But what does it mean for something to be conceivable or inconceivable, and by whom? It is easy to conceive of something other than oxygen in the place of oxygen, if one does not know anything about oxygen. In that much, knowledge and science constrain imagination—although, no doubt, also help to focus it. The interplay between knowledge and imagination is most problematic when the 'knowledge' is wrong.

In any case, until very recently, most human societies did not mark a strict divide between imagination and belief, or

Imagination

fiction and reality, with each one informing and enriching the other. In fact, it could be argued that, in many important respects, the fiction primed over the reality—and even that this has been, and no doubt still is, one of the hallmarks of *homo sapiens*. Today, there are potent pills for people who confuse imaginings and beliefs, but back in the day no one ever thought that life, despite its much harder hardships, might be meaningless—which I think tells us quite a bit about imagination and its uses, and also, incidentally, about mental illness and its causes.

The uses of imagination are many, more than I can enumerate. Most children begin to develop pretend play at around fifteen months of age. What are children doing when they pretend play? And why are they so absorbed in works of imagination? When I was seven years old, I would devour book after book and plead with my parents for those not already in the bookcase. By playing out scenarios and extending themselves beyond their limited experience, children seek to make sense of the world and find their place within it. This meaning-making is full of emotion—joy, excitement, awe—which finds an echo in every subsequent act of creation.

Whenever we look at an object such as the Mona Lisa, we see much more than just the frame and the brushstrokes. In fact, we barely see the brushstrokes at all. In imagination as in our dreams, we ascribe form, pattern, and significance to things, and then reflect them back onto those things. Without this work of interpreting and assimilating, the world would be no more than an endless stream of sense impressions, as it might sometimes seem to those who lack imagination, with no hope of escape or reprieve.

More than that, by imagination we are able to complete the world, or our world, by conjuring up the missing parts, and even to inhabit entirely other worlds such as Middle-earth or the Seven Kingdoms. Imagination remains highly active throughout adulthood, and what is chick lit or even pornography if not an aid to the adult imagination? In one year (2018), Pornhub recorded 33.5 billion visits, equivalent to more than four times the world population—and that's just on the one site.

If imagination lets us feel at home in the world, it also enables us to get things done in the world. Science advances by hypothesis, which is a function of imagination, and philosophy makes frequent use of thought experiments such as the brain in the vat, the trolley problem, and Plato's Republic. More than that, imagination enables us to form associations and connections, and thereby to apply our knowledge to real life situations. It opens up alternatives and possibilities and guides our decision-making by playing them out in our mind. So many of our failures—and, dare I say, a few of our successes—are in fact failures of the imagination.

Imagination also enables us to talk to one another, understand one another, and work together. Without it, there could be no metaphor, no irony, no humour, no past or future tense, and no conditional either. Indeed, there could be no language at all, for what are words if not symbols and representations?

By imagination, we can put ourselves in other people's shoes, think what they think, feel what they feel, and project them and our relationship into the future. Problems in autism, which can be understood as a disorder of imagination, include abnormalities in patterns of communication, impairments in social interactions, and a restricted repertoire of behaviours, interests, and activities.

Imagination is the highest form of thought, and almost divine in its reach. With enough imagination, we could identify and solve all of our problems. With enough imagination, we would never have to work again—or, at least, not for money. With enough imagination, we could win over, or defeat, anyone we wanted to. But our imagination is so poor that we haven't even imagined what it would be like to have that much imagination.

I'm lucky to have received a decent education, but one thing it certainly didn't do for me is cultivate my imagination. In fact, medical school in particular did everything it could to destroy it. In recent years, I've been trying to recover the bright and vivid imagination that I left behind in primary school. For that, I've been doing just three things, all of them very simple—or, at least, very simple to explain:

- Being more aware of the importance of imagination. Making time for sleep and idleness.
- Taking inspiration from the natural world.

179

I'll conclude briefly with these few words from William Blake, which point to the significance of the natural world and the transcending power of imagination:

> *The tree which moves some to tears of joy is in the eyes of others only a green thing that stands in the way. Some see nature all ridicule and deformity... and some scarce see nature at all. But to the eyes of the man of imagination, nature is imagination itself.*

Final words

Well, that was a whirlwind, ten years of thinking, two years of writing, and I'm going to wrap up with just three thoughts...

The highest purpose of education is to unlearn what we once took for granted, to replace certainty with subtlety, prejudice with compassion, and destiny with possibility. If reason is slippery, knowledge is even more so. The oracle at Delphi called Socrates the wisest of all people because Socrates knew how little he knew. So instead of running around thinking that we know things, giving up our lives to those things and making trouble in the world, we would do better to sit down a bit, recognizing just how muddled we are and, if we are not in England, enjoying some sunshine at the same time.

The kōan is a paradox or riddle that encourages the zen apprentice to connect the dots by subverting the rational and egotistic mind. Although seen as a paradigm of reason and philosophy, no one could be more kōan-like than Socrates. But our culture equates thinking with logical reasoning, and strength with knowledge, and this has done, and continues to do, untold harm. Instead of digging ourselves in deeper, we ought to be rehabilitating alternative forms of cognition that can be used to support, supplement, or supplant logical reasoning and return us to wholeness. Our reservoir of madness, often perceived as the polar opposite of reason, is a precious resource that we can learn not merely to control but to exploit, or to control by exploiting.

An intuition involves a coming together of loosely linked facts, concepts, experiences, thoughts, and feelings, and we can encourage intuition by tearing down the psychological barriers that are keeping them apart. If intuition involves stepping back from our person, so does wisdom, insight, imagination, and even reason. What usually gets in the way of both reason and non-rational forms of cognition is not stupidity as such, or feeble-mindedness, but fear and the thing that fear protects, that is, our self-esteem, our sense of self, our ego. If we are to unleash our full cognitive and human potential, we need to love life more than we fear it, we need to suppress or destroy our ego, to *commit metaphorical suicide*—which will be the work of a life well spent. In the Athenian prison, shortly before drinking the hemlock, Socrates told his friends that absolute justice, absolute beauty, and absolute good cannot be apprehended with the eyes or any other bodily organ, but only by the mind or soul. Therefore, the philosopher [Greek, 'lover of wisdom'] seeks in as far as possible to separate body from soul and become pure, unindividuated soul. As death is the complete separation of body and soul, the philosopher aims at death, and can be said to be almost dead.

And so, if we are to live, we must first learn to die.

Notes

Introduction
- Carl Jung, *Memories, Dreams, Reflections* (1961).
- Diogenes Laertius, *Lives of Eminent Philosophers*, Bk VI.
- RD Laing, *The Politics of Experience* (1967), Ch 1.

Chapter 2: Fallacies
- Hillary Clinton, National Security Speech Delivered at Balboa Park, San Diego, California, 2 June 2016.
- Donald Trump, Third Presidential Debate, 20 October 2016.
- Donald Trump on Twitter (@realDonaldTrump), 18 November 2017.
- Michael Gove, during an interview with Faisal Islam on Sky News, June 3, 2016.
- Theresa May, at various times during her prime ministership.

Chapter 6: Rhetoric
- Fugees (1996), *Zealots*.
- Edgar Allen Poe (1845), *The Raven*.
- Alexander Pope (1734), *An Essay on Man: Epistle II*.
- John Milton (1671), *Samson Agonistes I. 80*.

185

- Shakespeare (1597), *Romeo and Juliette II, 2.*
- Bible, Romans 5:4 (KJV).
- Shakespeare (1609), Sonnet 116.
- Francis Thompson (1893), *The Hound of Heaven.*
- Lyndon Johnson, Special Message to the Congress: The American Promise, March 15, 1965.
- William (Bill) Jefferson Clinton, Oklahoma Bombing Memorial Prayer Service Address, April 23, 1995.
- Abraham Lincoln, Second Inaugural Address, March 4, 1865.
- Bible, Revelation 22:13 (KJV).
- Lady Caroline Lamb, to describe Lord Byron.
- Bible, Matthew 19:30 (KJV).
- Bible, Matthew 7:6 (KJV).
- Book of Common Prayer (1549), Psalm 24.
- Horace, *Odes* 3, 21.
- Virgil, *Aeneid* 2, 353. *Moriamur, et in media arma ruamus.*
- Henry Peacham (1577), *The Garden of Eloquence.*
- Flanders & Swann (1959), *Have Some Madeira, M'Dear.*
- Winston Churchill, speech to the Commons, June 4, 1940.
- The Police (1983), *Every Breath You Take.*
- Shakespeare, Hamlet, III, 1.
- Shakespeare, Timon of Athens, III, 4.
- Shakespeare, Antony and Cleopatra, II, 5.
- Bible, Song of Solomon 1:2 (KJV).
- Elvis Presley (1956), *Love Me Tender.*
- Attributed to George Bernard Shaw. *What a pity that youth...*
- Bible, Ecclesiastes 3:2 (KJV).

Chapter 7: Language
- Kenneth Grahame (1895), *The Golden Age, Lusisti Satis.*
- Ludwig Wittgenstein (1922), *Tractatus Logico-Philosophicus* 5.6.
- One language dies every two weeks. Stated by the UN Secretary General at the opening of the 10th Session of the UN Permanent Forum on Indigenous Issues. May 16, 2011.
- Walt Whitman, *Leaves of Grass, Song of the Universal.*
- Winawer J et al. (2007): *Russian Blues Reveal Effects of Language on Color Discrimination.* Proc Natl Acad Sci USA 104(19):7780–5.
- Fausey CM et al. (2010): *Constructing Agency: The Role of Language.* Front Psychol 1:162.
- Boroditsky L et al. (2003): *Sex, Syntax, and Semantics.* In *Language and Mind: Advances in the Study of Language and Cognition*, ed. Genter D & Goldin-Meadow S, pp. 61–80. Cambridge University Press.
- George Lakoff (1987): *Women, Fire, and Dangerous Things: What Categories Reveal About the Mind.* University of Chicago Press.
- Segel E & Boroditsky L (2010): *Grammar in Art.* Front Psychol. 1:244.
- Bylund E & Athanasopoulos P (2017): *The Whorfian Time Warp: Representing Duration Through the Language Hourglass.* J Exp Psychol Gen. 146(7):911–916.
- Gaby A (2012): *The Thaayorre Think of Time Like They Talk of Space.* Front Psychol 3:300.

Chapter 8: Languages
- Giovanni Carlo Scaramelli, Venetian Ambassador in England, in a letter to the Doge and Senate. April 7, 1603.
- Theresa May, Keynote Speech to the Conservative Party Conference, October 5, 2016.
- Poarch G & Bialystok E (2015): *Bilingualism as a Model for Multitasking.* Dev Rev 35:113–124.
- Lauchlan F et al. (2012): *Bilingualism in Sardinia and Scotland: Exploring the Cognitive Benefits of Speaking a 'Minority' Language.* International Journal of Bilingualism 17(1):43–56.
- Blom E et al. (2014): *The Benefits of Being Bilingual: Working Memory in Bilingual Turkish-Dutch Children.* Journal of Experimental Child Psychology 128:105–119.
- Abutalebi J et al. (2012): *Bilingualism Tunes the Anterior Cingulate Cortex For Conflict Monitoring.* Cereb Cortex 22(9):2076–86.
- Samuels WE et al. (2016): *Executive Functioning Predicts Academic Achievement in Middle School: A Four-Year Longitudinal Study.* Journal of Educational Research 109(5):478–490.
- Costa A et al. (2014): *Your Morals Depend on Your Language.* PLoS One 9(4):e94842.
- Bialystok E et al. (2007): *Bilingualism as a Protection Against the Onset of Symptoms of Dementia.* Neuropsychologia 45:459–464.
- Perani D et al. (2017): *The Impact of Bilingualism on Brain Reserve and Metabolic Connectivity in Alzheimer's Dementia.* Proc Natl Acad Sci USA 114(7):1690–1695.

- Alladi S et al. (2016): *Impact of Bilingualism on Cognitive Outcome After Stroke.* Stroke 47(1):258–61.
- Johnson: *What is a Foreign Language Worth?* The Economist, March 11, 2014.
- Agirdag O (2014): *The Long-Term Effects of Bilingualism on Children of Immigration: Student Bilingualism and Future Earnings.* International Journal of Bilingual Education and Bilingualism 17(4):449–464.
- Grin F et al. (2009): *Langues etrangères dans l'activité professionnelle, projet no. 405640-108630.* Geneva: University of Geneva.
- *Language Skills Deficit Costs the UK £48bn a Year.* Lucy Pawle, The Guardian, December 10, 2013.
- Ervin-Tripp S (1964): *An Analysis of the Interaction of Language, Topic, and Listener.* American Anthropologist 66:86–102.
- Ludwig Wittgenstein (1953), *Philosophical Investigations*, 115. Trans. G Anscombe 1958.
- Cunningham TH & Graham CR (2000): *Increasing Native English Vocabulary Recognition Through Spanish Immersion: Cognate Transfer From Foreign to First Language.* Journal of Educational Psychology 92(1):37–49.
- Robert Aickman (1966): *Powers of Darkness: Macabre Stories, The Wine-Dark Sea.* London. Collins.

Chapter 9: Reason
- The Universal Declaration of Human Rights, adopted by the United Nations General Assembly on December 10, 1948.
- Bible, John 1:1 (KJV).
- René Descartes (1673), *Discourse on the Method*.
- 'God gave all the easy problems to the physicists' has been attributed to James March.
- Aristotle, *On Generation and Corruption*.
- Plato, *Lesser Hippias*.
- Plato, *Protagoras*.
- Jancis Robinson on Twitter (@JancisRobinson): BTW what qualifies someone to call themselves a sommelier, do you think? (Lights touch paper...) February 2, 2019.
- Blaise Pascal (1670), *Pensées*, 267.
- Plato, *Cratylus*. Trans. Benjamin Jowett.

Chapter 10: Intelligence
- Salovey P & Mayer JD (1990): *Emotional intelligence*. Imagination, Cognition and Personality 9(3):185–211.
- Plato, *Republic*.
- Aristotle, *Nicomachean Ethics*, Bk 10.
- Rudyard Kipling (1902), *The White Man's Burden*.
- Rees MJ & Earles JA (1992): *Intelligence is the Best Predictor of Job Performance*. Current Directions in Psychological Science 1(3):86–89.
- Saxon W (1989): *Obituary William B Shockley, 79, Creator of Transistor and Theory on Race*. New York Times, August 14, 1989.

Chapter 11: Knowledge
- Ohayon MM (2000): *Prevalence of Hallucinations and Their Pathological Associations in the General Population.* Psychiatry Research 97(2-3):153–64.
- Plato, *Meno.*
- CB Broad, *The Philosophy of Francis Bacon: An Address Delivered at Cambridge on the Occasion of the Bacon Tercentenary.* October 5, 1926.
- CA Strong (1923), *A Theory of Knowledge*, p. xi. New York: The Macmillan Company.
- Gettier EL (1963): *Is Justified True Belief Knowledge?* Analysis 23:121–123.
- Plato, *Republic*, Bk VII. Trans. Benjamin Jowett.

Chapter 12: Memory
- Diogenes Laertius, *Lives of Eminent Philosophers*, Bk III, *Plato.*
- John Barth (1958): *The Remobilization of Jacob Horner.* Short story published in Esquire Magazine.
- BBC (2019): *Thatcher: A Very British Revolution*, Pt 5.
- Loftus EF & Palmer JC (1974): *Reconstruction of Automobile Destruction: An Example of the Interaction Between Language and Memory.* Journal of Verbal Learning and Verbal Behavior 13(5):585–589.
- Marcel Proust (1913-27), *Remembrance of Things Past, Vol 1: Swann's Way: Within a Budding Grove,* pp48–51. The definitive French Pleiade edition translated by Scott Moncrieff and Terence Kilmartin. New York: Vintage.
- Albert Einstein, as quoted in *Journal of France and Germany (1942–1944)* by Gilbert Fowler White, in

excerpt published in *Living with Nature's Extremes: The Life of Gilbert Fowler White* (2006) by Robert E Hinshaw.
- Oscar Wilde (1890), *The Picture of Dorian Gray*, Ch 8.
- Lane DM & Chang YA (2018): *Chess Knowledge Predicts Chess Memory Even After Controlling for Chess Experience: Evidence for the Role of High-level Processes*. Memory and Cognition 46(3):337–348.

Chapter 13: Science
- Lexchin J et al. (2003): *Pharmaceutical Industry Sponsorship and Research Outcome and Quality: Systematic Review*. BMJ 326:1167–1170.
- NR Hanson, *On Observation*. In TJ McGrew et al. (2009), *The Philosophy of Science: An Historical Anthology*, p 432.
- Max Planck (1949), *Scientific Autobiography and Other Papers*.
- Thomas Kuhn (1962), *The Structure of Scientific Revolutions*.
- Paul Feyerabend (1975), *Against Method*.
- Paul Feyerabend (1991), *Who's Who in America*.

Chapter 14: Truth
- Plato, *Cratylus*.
- Bible, John 8:32 (KJV).
- Rudy Giuliani during a *Meet the Press* interview on August 18, 2018, discussing the fear that Donald Trump could 'get trapped into perjury' under special-counsel questioning.

- Kellyanne Conway during a *Meet the Press* interview on January 22, 2017, defending Sean Spicer's false statement about the attendance numbers at Donald Trump's inauguration.
- Michael Gove during an interview with Faisal Islam on Sky News, June 3, 2016.
- Søren Kierkegaard (1850), *The Diary of Søren Kierkegaard*, 5, 3, 128.
- Harry Frankfurt (2005), *The Importance of Bullshit*, *The Importance of What We Care About*.
- Aristotle, *Metaphysics*, IV, vii.
- Avicenna, *Kitab Al-Shifa The Book of Healing*, I, viii.
- Aquinas (1485), *Summa Theologiae* I, 16, 1, and *De Veritate* 1, 1.
- Martin Heidegger (1943), *On the Essence of Truth*. Trans. John Sallis.
- William James (1909), *The Meaning of Truth*, Preface.
- Friedrich Nietzsche (1886), *Beyond Good and Evil*, 333.

Chapter 15: Intuition
- Aristotle, *Rhetoric*.
- Aristotle, *Poetics*.
- Plato, *Phaedo*.
- Plato, *Phaedrus*.
- Plato, *Meno*.

Chapter 16: Wisdom
- Bible, Ecclesiastes 7:12 (KJV)
- Plato, *Lysis*.
- Seneca the Younger, *Epistles*, 13.

- Bible, Proverbs 11:2 (KJV).
- Shakespeare (1603), *As You Like It*, V, 1.
- Plato, *Apology*.
- Confucius, as quoted in Henry David Thoreau (1954), *Walden*, Ch 1.
- *Dhammapada: The Sayings of the Buddha*. Trans. John Richards (1993).
- Plato, *Meno*.
- Aristotle, *Metaphysics*, Alpha.
- Cicero, *Tusculan Disputations*, 3, 30.
- Robert Nozick (1989), *The Examined Life: Philosophical Meditations*, 23.
- Plato, *Protagoras*.
- Bible, Luke 23:34 (KJV).
- John Milton (1667), *Paradise Lost*, Bk I.

Chapter 17: Inspiration
- Homer, *Iliad*, first lines.
- Bible, 2 Peter 1:21 (KJV).
- Thomas Edison (1902), as quoted in the September 1932 issue of *Harper's Monthly Magazine*.
- Plato, *Ion*.
- Plato, *Phaedrus*.
- Seneca (~60), *de Tranquillitate Animi*.
- Shakespeare, *A Midsummer Night's Dream*, V, 1.
- John Dryden (1681): *Absalom and Achitophel*, I, 150–164.
- André Gide, *Journal 1889–1939, Septembre 1894*. Trans. Neel Burton. Les choses les plus belles sont celles que souffle la folie et qu'écrit la raison. Il faut demeurer entre

les deux, tout près de la folie quand on rêve, tout près de la raison quand on écrit.

Chapter 18: Insight
- Leon Festinger (1956), *When Prophecy Fails*.
- The earliest known version of the rabbit-duck illusion is an unattributed drawing from the 23 October 1892 issue of *Fliegende Blätter*, a German humour magazine. It was made famous by Wittgenstein, who included it in his *Philosophical Investigations*.
- Nyhan B & Reifler J (2015): *Does Correcting Myths About the Flu Vaccine Work? An Experimental Evaluation of the Effects of Corrective Information*. Vaccine 33(3):459–464.
- Kekulé first mentioned the snake dream in an extemporaneous speech at a benzene symposium in 1890.

Chapter 19: Emotion
- Quoted in Marcel Haedrich (1972): *Coco Chanel: Her Life, Her Secrets*, Ch 1. Trans. Charles Lam Markmann. Little Brown and Co.
- Gustave Flaubert (1950), *Madame Bovary*, p120. Trans. A. Russell. Harmondsworth: Penguin.
- William James (1884): *What is an Emotion?* 9, 188–205.
- Ibid.
- David Hume (1738): *A Treatise of Human Nature* II.3.3, 415.
- Aristotle, *Nicomachean Ethics*, Bk 10. Trans. WD Ross.

- Discussing the number of Tory candidates who had attended Oxbridge in the BBC's *Newsnight*, Jacob Rees-Mogg said: 'The Tory party, when it's elected, has to be able to form a government and it's not going to be able to form a government if it has potted plants as candidates simply to make up quotas.' October 4, 2006.
- Hugh Kingsmill (1938), *D.H. Lawrence*, Ch 2.

Chapter 20: Music
- Bible, 1 Samuel 16:23 (KJV).
- Plato, *Republic* Bk IV. Trans. Benjamin Jowett.
- Aristotle, *Politics* Bk VIII. Trans. Benjamin Jowett.
- Salimpoor VN et al. (2011): *Anatomically Distinct Dopamine Release During Anticipating and Experience of Peak Emotion to Music.* Nature Neuroscience, published online January 9, 2011.
- Malik A et al. (2017): *Anhedonia to Music and Mu-Opioids: Evidence from the Administration of Naltrexone.* Scientific Reports, published online February 8, 2017.
- Chanda ML & Levitin DJ (2013): *The Neurochemistry of Music.* Trends in Cognitive Sciences 17(4):179–193.
- Bradt J et al (2013): *Music for Stress and Anxiety Reduction in Coronary Heart Disease Patients.* Cochrane Database Syst Rev. 12: CD006577.
- Aalbers S et al. (2017): *Music Therapy for Depression.* Cochrane Database Syt Rev. 11: CD004517.
- Sherratt K et al. (2004): *Music Interventions for people with dementia: A Review of the Literature.* Ageing & Mental Health 8(1):3–12.

- Magee WL et al. (2017): *Music Interventions for Acquired Brain Injury*. Cochrane Database Syt Rev. 1: CD006787.
- Ravindra A et al. (2012): *Maternal Music Exposure during Pregnancy Influences Neonatal Behaviour: An Open-Label Randomized Controlled Trial.* Int J Pediatr, published online February 14, 2012.

Chapter 21: Imagination
- Albert Einstein, in an interview by George Sylvester Viereck for the *Saturday Evening Post*, October 26, 1929.
- David Hume (1738), *A Treatise of Human Nature*, I.2.2.
- Pornhub Insights, *2018 Year in Review*. December 11, 2018.
- William Blake (1799), *Letter to Revd. Dr Trusler*.

Final words
- Plato, *Apology*.
- Plato, *Meno*.
- Plato, *Phaedo*.

Index

abduction, 87, 108
ad hominem, 8
advertising, 94
affirming the consequent, 4, 108
Aickman, Robert, 64
Al Farabi, 172
allegory of the cave, see *Plato's cave*
alliteration, 39
alternative facts, 115
Alzheimer's disease, see *dementia*
anadiplosis, 40
anaphora, 41, 44
analogical fallacy, 10
anastrophe, 43
Anaxagoras, 135
Ancient Greek, 52, 67
anger, 34, 172
animals, 51, 68, 73, 77, 84, 93, 124, 154, 158, 159, 161
antiphrasis, 46
antithesis, 46
antitimeria, 45
antonomasia, 48
anxiety, see *fear*

apatheia, 154
apathy, 71
appeal to hypocrisy, 8
appeal to popularity, 9
Aquinas, 117
Archimedes, 149–150
arguments, 1–5, 7, 37, 68, 72, 87, 166
argument from ignorance, 11
argument to moderation, 9
Aristotle, 67, 71, 72, 78, 79, 107, 117, 124, 128, 135, 137, 145, 165, 172, 173
artificial intelligence, 80
artists (see also, *poets, poetry*), 135, 144
Athena, 132
autism, 179
Avicenna, 117

bad news, 137–139
Barth, John, 98
basic emotions, 158–161, 162
Bassa (language), 50
Beck, Aaron, 35
begging the question, 11

benzene molecule, 152
bifurcation, 9
bilingualism, 59–65
Blake, William, 180
blue, shades of, 51–52
brain in a vat, 83
brain injury, 71, 95, 153, 174
brainwashing, 94
Brexit, 8, 9, 10, 60, 98, 169
Buddha, the, 134
bullshit, 116–117

Carlin, George, 63
catachresis, 45
catastrophic thinking, 35
catharsis, 173–174
Chanel, Coco, 157
Charlemagne, 63
Charles V, 63
cherry picking, 106
Chesteron, GK, 124
chiasmus, 42
children, 51, 57, 60, 149, 158, 159, 177
Christie, Agatha, 99
Churchill, Winston, 38, 44
Cicero, 135–136, 145
Cleopatra, 115
Clinton, Hillary, 8
cogency (logic), 3
cognitive behavioural therapy, 35
cognitive bias, 34–35
cognitive distortion, 35–36
coherence theory of truth, 118, 119

colour terms, 50
computer scientists, 78
confabulation, 96–97, 98
confirmation bias, 35
confounding factors, 106
Confucius, 134
consonance, 38
correspondence bias, 34
correspondence theory of truth, 117, 119
Conway, Kellyanne, 115
courage, 136–137, 172
Cratylus, the, 67, 115
creativity, 49, 103, 142
cynic, cynical, xi
cum hoc, 10, 19

Dædalus, 86
Dalai Lama, the, 120
Dani (language), 50
data dredging, 106
death, xi, 32, 56, 97, 111, 133, 135, 156, 182
debating, 73
declarative knowledge, 85
déjà-vu, 98
Delphic oracle, 133
dementia, 61, 77, 95–97, 174
denying the antecedent, 5
depression, 35, 36, 71, 103, 137, 153
Descartes, 68, 87
desires, 71
diacope, 40
Diogenes the Cynic, x–xi

Index

displacement, 34
dissociation, 99
double pendulum, 70
dreaming, 146
drug trials, 106
Dryden, 145
Dyribal (language), 55

echo chamber, 35
Edison, Thomas, 142
education, xiv, 69, 71, 73, 80, 90, 97, 123, 128, 134–135, 137, 142–143, 153, 179, 181
egocentricity (in languages), 53
ego defence(s) (see also, *self-deception*), 31–34
Einstein, 101, 175
Ekman, Paul, 158
Elizabeth I of England, 59–60
emotional intelligence, 78
emotions, 33, 71, 98, 107, 120, 121, 137, 151, 153–170, 172, 173, 175
enallage, 46
English (language), 53, 54, 55, 56, 57, 62, 63
envy, 22, 34, 156
epanalepsis, 10
epinephrine, 98, 163
epistrophe, 37, 41
epizeuxis, 39
Ervin-Tripp, Susan, 62
ethics, see *virtue*
Euathlus, 72–73
European Union, 8, 9, 10

evidentiality, 54
existential anxiety, 32
experiments (science), 106
expressions of emotion, 161–162
eyewitness testimony, 99

fake news, 115–116
fallacies, 4–11, 31
falsification, see *Popper, Karl*
fear, xii, 32, 33, 71, 121, 125, 137, 156, 163, 164, 173, 182
feelings, 155
Festinger, Leon, 150
Feyerabend, Paul, 112–113
Flaubert, Gustave, 160–161
flu jab, 152
Foucault, Michel, 117
Frankfurt, Harry, 116–117
free will, 21, 23
French, 54, 55, 63, 83, 94, 141
Freud, ix, x, 23, 110

gambler's fallacy, 10
Game of Thrones, 93
gender (grammar), 55, 56
genetic fallacy, 8, 115
genius, 80–81
Gettier, Edmund, 88
German, 50, 55, 56, 63, 152
Gide, André, 145
Giuliani, Rudy, 115
God (see also, *religion*), 11, 21, 32, 51, 67, 71, 79, 109, 115, 127, 135, 141
Gove, Michael, 8, 115

201

Grahame, Kenneth, 49
grammar (see also, *language*), 53–56, 57
Greek (Modern), 51–52, 57
guilt, 34

hallucinations, 84
Hanlon's razor, 109
Hanson, NR, 107
happiness, 67, 79
Hebrew, 57
Heidegger, Martin, 118
hendiadys, 47
Hobson's choice, 9
Holy Ghost, 141
Homer, 52, 141, 143, 171
Homo sapiens, 132
horror films, 158
Hume, David, 165, 176
hunter-gatherers, 59, 77
hypallage, 43
hyperbaton, 43
hyperheaven, 78
hypersanity, ix–xiv
hypozeuxis, 44
hysteron proteron, 43

idealization, 32, 98
illusions, 84
induction, problem of, 70, 87–88, 107–110
insight, 149–152, 182
imagination, 103, 175–180, 182
infinity, 74
inspiration, 141–148

instinct, 68, 124
intellectualization, 32–34
intelligence, 77–81
Internet, the, 59, 70, 78, 85, 115, 131
intuition, 68, 120, 123–129, 182
Ion, the, 143–144
IQ, 78, 80–81
isocolon, 32

James-Lange theory, 162–163
Japanese, 53, 62
jargon, 53
jealousy, 36
Jesus, 115, 136, 154
John the Apostle, 115
judgement, 69, 118, 172
Jung, CG, ix–x, 144
justification, 86–87
justified true belief, 85–86

Kant, 79
Kekulé, 152
Kierkegaard, 116
Kipling, Rudyard, 79–80
know-how, 85, 94
knowledge, 73, 77, 83–91, 94, 96, 107–108, 113, 126, 127, 132, 133–135, 136, 175, 176, 178, 181
kōan (Zen), 125–126, 127, 181
Korsakov syndrome, 95
Kuhn, Thomas, 110–111, 111–112
Kuuk Thaayorre (language), 57

Index

Laing, RD, ix, x, xii
Lakatos, Imre, 111–112
Lakoff, George, 55
language, 36, 36–65, 68, 73–74, 78, 107, 117, 119, 159, 162, 164, 178
Latin, 53, 63, 78
Lesser Hippias, the, 72
leucotomy, 111
library, 58
lies, 116–117, 121
lizard, 158–159
Locke, John, 128, 147
logical fallacies, see *fallacies*
logic, logical reasoning (see also, *reason*), xiii, 40, 68, 69, 116
logos, 67
love, 32, 52, 113, 124, 155, 160–161
Lysis, the, 48, 131–132

madness, ix–x, xii, xiii, 16, 17, 35, 36, 71, 86, 118, 127, 136, 144–145, 177, 182
Mark Antony, 115
Mauritius, 158
May, Theresa, 60
meaning, 97
medical research, 32
medical student(s), 32, 110
medicine, 72, 108, 109, 110, 111
memory (see also, *dementia*), 93–103, 174, 176
Meno, the, 86, 127–128, 134–135

mental disorder, see *madness*
metaphors, 57
metonymy, 47
Milton, John, 139
Mimir, 132
mnemonics, 102
Mnemosyne, 96, 141, 145
Moniz, Egas, 111
monkeys, 49
motivation, 142
multiculturalism, 60
multilingualism, 59–65
muses, the, 96, 141, 171
music, 37, 171–174
music therapy, 172–174

Newton's laws, 112, 113
Nicomachean Ethics, the, 79, 128, 165
Nietzsche, 118
nostalgia, 96–97, 98
noun classes, 55
Nozick, Robert, 136

Obama, Barack, 37
Ockham's razor, 109
Odin, 132
owl, 132
Oxford, 13, 78, 110, 168
oxymoron, 46

Papua New Guinea, 59
paradigms (science), 110–111, 113, 151
paradox, 46

203

parallelism, 42
parrhesia, x
Pascal, Blaise, 75
passions, the, 71, 154
pendulum, 70
periodic sentence, 44
personal pronouns, 54
personification, 56
perspective (see also, *wisdom*), 33, 135-139
Phaedrus, the, 52, 126-127, 144
philosopher kings, 78
philosophy, 87, 91, 126, 131, 178, 182
physics, 71, 74, 105
Planck, Max, 111
plants, 77, 149, 179-180
Plato, 48, 52, 67, 72, 73, 78, 86, 97, 115, 126-128, 131-132, 143-144, 171-172, 178
Plato's cave, 83, 89-91
ploce, 40
Plutchik, Robert, 158, 159, 160
poets, poetry, 37, 50, 123, 135, 143-144
politics, 13, 37, 56, 60, 72-73, 75, 78, 79-80, 90, 98, 115-116, 117, 118, 126, 128, 131, 165, 169
polyptoton, 40
Pope, the, 119
Popper, Karl, 70, 109-110, 111
pornography, 178
Portuguese, 48
pleonasm, 42

pragmatic theory of truth, 118-119
present perfect tense, 53
procedural memory, 93
projection, 31-32
prospective memory, 95
Protagoras, 72-73
Protagoras, the, 73
Proust, Marcel, 100
psychagogia, 52
psychiatry, ix, 32, 33, 96, 151
publication bias, 106
pun, 45
Pythagoras' theorem, 128

quantum theory, 74

racism, 79-80, 81, 118
rational thought, see *reason*
reason (see also, *logic*), 31, 33, 67-75, 77, 79, 83, 88, 96, 111, 116, 123, 125, 126, 128-129, 145, 151, 153, 165, 178, 181, 182
red herring, 7
religion (see also, *God*), 105, 112, 119, 153
REM sleep, 146
repression, 32
Republic, the, 78-79, 171-172, 198
resonance, 39
rhetoric, 37-48, 49, 52
Rhetoric, the, 71, 124
Robinson, Jancis, 74

rollercoasters, 158
Rumi, 51
runaway train, 11
Russian, 51–52, 54–55

sadomasochism, 158
SATs, 79
saudade, 48
scapegoating, 34
science, 105–113, 116, 125, 128, 132, 134, 151, 178
scientific method, 105–106
Schadenfreude, 156, 160
Schockley, William, 80–81
Schopenhauer, 23, 173
science, 33, 70, 86, 105–113, 119–120, 131, 175, 176
Sehnsucht, 50
selective abstraction, 35
self-deception, 31–34, 71, 84–85, 98, 120–121, 156, 164, 165, 168, 182
self-esteem, 35
self-referential statements, 74
Seneca, 133, 145
senses, the, 74, 83, 84, 99, 107, 135, 177, 182
Shakespeare, 134, 145
sibilance, 39, 48
sight, sense of, 83, 107, 132
silence, 50
Simpson, Homer, 150
Skinner, BF, xiv
sleep, 95, 101, 125, 146, 179
smell, sense of, 99–100

snobbery, 166–170
Socrates, 48, 72, 73, 78, 115, 120, 126–128, 131–132, 132–133, 134–135, 136, 143–144, 181, 182
Socratic method, 78, 127
sommelier, 74, 167
sophists, 72–73
soundness (logic), 3, 4
Spanish, 53, 54, 55, 57, 64
stoics, stoicism, 10
straw man, 7
stress, 98–99
stroke, 62
surprise, 157
Swedish, 57
syllepsis, 44
symbolism, 49
symploce, 41
synedoche, 48
syntax, 53

tautology, 42
tears, 163–164
tense (grammar), 54
Terman Study, 81
testimonial knowledge, 84–85, 94
Thatcher, Margaret, 97
theory of relativity, 74, 112
Thinking Skills Assesssment, the, 13
thou (pronoun), 55
three-body problems, 70–71
time, 152

205

time (in language), 57
tragedy, 173–174
traits, 156–157
translation, 63
tricolon, 42
tripartite theory, 86, 88
Trump, Donald, 8, 78, 115, 116, 169
truth, 68, 73, 83, 113, 115–121, 123, 124, 128
Turkish, 54

uh-oh moments, 150
Universal Declaration of Human Rights, the, 67
universals (Plato), 144, 182

validity (logic), 2, 4, 68
virtue, 73, 127, 134–135, 142, 156, 165, 166, 172

Welch, Jack, 152
Whitman, Walt, 50
Wilde, Oscar, 102
wine, 7, 10, 46, 74, 167, 168
wisdom, 109, 128, 131–139, 142, 182
Wittgenstein, 50, 63
women, 56, 79–80

Zen Buddhism, 125–126
Zeno's paradoxes, 74
zeugma, 43

By the same author

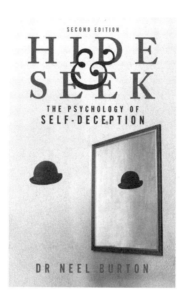

Hide and Seek: The Psychology of Self-Deception
ISBN 978-0-9929127-9-6

Self-deception is common and universal, and the cause of most human tragedies. Of course, the science of self-deception can help us to live better and get more out of life. But it can also cast a murky light on human nature and the human condition, for example, on such exclusively human phenomena as anger, depression, fear, pity, pride, dream making, love making, and god making, not to forget age-old philosophical problems such as selfhood, virtue, happiness, and the good life. Nothing, in the end, could possibly be more important.

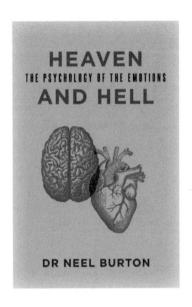

Heaven and Hell: The Psychology of the Emotions
ISBN 978-0-9929127-2-7

Many people lumber through life without giving full consideration to their emotions, partly because our empirical, materialistic culture does not encourage it or even make it seem possible, and partly because it requires unusual strength to gaze into the abyss of our deepest drives, needs, and fears. This book proposes to do just that, examining over 25 emotions ranging from lust to love and humility to humiliation, and drawing some powerful and astonishing conclusions along the way.

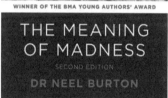

The Meaning of Madness
ISBN 978-0-9929127-3-4

This book aims to open up the debate on mental disorders, to get people interested and talking, and to get them thinking. For example, what is schizophrenia? Why is it so common? Why does it affect human beings but not other animals? What might this tell us about our mind and body, language and creativity, music and religion? What are the boundaries between mental disorder and 'normality'? Is there a relationship between mental disorder and genius? These are some of the difficult but important questions that this book confronts, with the overarching aim of exploring what mental disorders can teach us about human nature and the human condition.